DEC.  2C

Christian Publishing House

BIBLICAL STUDIES
Magazine

BIBLICAL STUDIES MAGAZINE

Biblical Studies Magazine is committed to providing our readers with tools and methods for better Bible study

Edward D. Andrews

Christian Publishing House

Cambridge, Ohio

CHRISTIAN PUBLISHING HOUSE
CONSERVATIVE CHRISTIAN BOOKS
APOLOGETIC DEFENSE OF GOD, THE FAITH, THE BIBLE, AND CHRISTIANITY

Copyright © 2018 Christian Publishing House

All rights reserved. Except for brief quotations in articles, other publications, book reviews, and blogs, no part of this book may be reproduced in any manner without prior written permission from the publishers. For information, write,

support@christianpublishers.org

Unless otherwise stated, scripture quotations are from The Holy Bible, Updated American Standard Version®, copyright © 2018 by Christian Publishing House, Professional Christian Publishing of the Good News. All rights reserved.

BIBLICAL STUDIES MAGAZINE

ISBN 13: 978-1-7906-3345-6

ISBN 10: 1-7906-3345-1

Table of Contents

MONTHLY DEVOTIONAL 6

How Is God Outside of or Beyond Time? 9
    Edward D. Andrews 9

Praying Unto God 13
    R. A. Torrey 13

NTTC John 5:4: Who Took John 5:4 Out of My Bible? 17
    Edward D. Andrews 17

The Bible Gives Us Answers to Questions about Life 21
    Edward D. Andrews 21

Hebrews 5:14 and 12:23: Why is The Greek teleios and teleioō translated differently? 25
    Edward D. Andrews 25

THE ATHEIST: Mistaken Views of Christianity, the Bible, and God 31
    Edward D. Andrews 31

YOUTH: Is There Anything Wrong with Flirting 34
    Edward D. Andrews 34

What Is Doubt 37
    Edward D. Andrews 37

Do Not Give Up in Your Walk with God! 50

Bibliography 62

MONTHLY DEVOTIONAL

December 2018

Be Wise and Accept Constructive Counsel

Proverbs 9:7-9 Updated American Standard Version (UASV)

⁷ He who corrects a scoffer gets himself abuse,
  and he who reproves a wicked man gets injury.[1]
⁸ Do not reprove a scoffer, or he will hate you;
  reprove a wise man, and he will love you.
⁹ Give instruction to a wise man, and he will be still wiser;
  teach[2] a righteous man, and he will increase in learning.

He who corrects a scoffer gets himself abuse: The verb translated **correct** (Heb. *yasar*) means to offer corrective counsel with the intention of improving the behavior of another. As discipline it need not come across as punishment, it is simply straight talk, withholding no punches, being very direct in teaching ones how to live their lives in the reverential fear of God so that they become wise from the life lessons before they are tempted by this wicked world and those alienated from God that would put them to the test.

The Hebrew word rendered **scoffer** (*lets*) is referring to someone who jeers, mocks, ridicules or treats someone with contempt. The person ridiculing another builds up resentment, anger, and hatred for the one trying to help make his path straight. Here the scoffer or ridiculer is one who resists being offered constructive correction and instruction. The **abuse** (Heb. *qalon*) is what one receives for his efforts at trying to give direction to a scoffer, which is utter contempt, disrespect, and dishonor.

And he who reproves a wicked man gets injury: This line is quite similar to the first line in meaning. **Reprove** (Heb. *yakach*) is similar in meaning to correct and has the same strong sense offering another straight talk, withholding no punches, being very direct in teaching ones how to live their life. The slight difference here with *yakach* **reprove** over *yasar* **correct** is that *yakach* carries a value judgment, implying that the one being reproved is guilty. When we look at the Hebrew word for wicked (*rasha*), we get the same implication of guilt, as the evil person is

---

[1] Lit *a blemish*
[2] Lit *make known to*

unrighteous, with a focus on the guilt of his being in violation of some standard.

Scoffers like to ridicule others, but if they are ridiculed themselves, they are unable to take it and will react badly, even violently. The wicked person has no appreciation for the one offering him reproof, to help him on the path of life. It can be very unwise to try and teach the beneficial truths of God's Word to someone who has utter contempt for you and the truth you are trying to share, for he will only ridicule your efforts. In your endeavor to reach the honest hearted with the good news of the kingdom, you need to be careful not to get too involved in debates and extensive argumentation with ridiculers.

Do not reprove a scoffer, or he will hate you: Reprove renders the same word that was used in 9:7b. **Scoffer** is as was used in 9:7a. **Scoffers** and **hate** are used in Proverbs 1:22, where the question is asked, "How long, O simple ones, will you love being simple-minded? And how long will scoffers delight in their scoffing and fools **hate knowledge**?"

Reprove a wise man, and he will love you: This line is the beginning of three lines (9:8b-9) that will contrast the first three lines of 9:7-8a. **Reprove** renders the same word from the previous line and that was used in 9:7b. Truly **wise** (Heb. *chakam*) **ones** can talk frankly to each other with straight talk, holding nothing back and help each other to improve or to correct themselves where needed. The wise has a capacity for insight, understanding, and discernment. Here **love you** has the sense of respecting you.

Give instruction to a wise man, and he will be still wiser: Why will a wise person love or respect you for giving him reproof? Because he knows that through correction "he will be still wiser."

Teach a righteous man, and he will increase in learning: Increase in learning is one who continues to take in knowledge. No one is too wise or too old to keep learning.

If we are to be taught by wisdom, there will be times when we must accept correction and reproof. Of course, most of us tend to bristle at such times, yet it becomes easier as we mature in the faith. A scoffer is a ridiculer, one who expresses derision or scorn about somebody or something. This one does not receive correction well at all and has a dislike of anyone so offering. The wicked are in a whole other category, as they are blinded by their hatred for others, especially anyone suggesting they need help.

Therefore, it is a waste of time to attempt to offer 'what is holy [Scriptural wisdom] to dogs or throw your pearls [Scriptural wisdom] in front of pigs, lest they trample them with their feet, and turn around and tear you to pieces.' (Matt. 7:6) These ones will only ridicule any attempt that we make at sharing the good news with them. We can look to the apostle Paul, who while teaching some Jews in Antioch, came across some, who just wanted to do nothing but contradict him. What was Paul's response? He told them "since you thrust [Scripture] aside and judge yourselves unworthy of eternal life, behold, we are turning to the Gentiles." Acts 13:45-46

There will come times when we are trying to share the good news, and they will look to just debate, criticize, and argue with us. If it is they alone, it would be best just to walk away, letting it be their loss. However, if it is a public place of some sort, and others are listening intently at how you answer the challenges, it may be best to offer a reasonable answer, then express that you are not here to argue, and walk away. If you had not offered the parting answer, the others may have thought you did not have an answer.

The Christian is to be different from the world of humankind that surrounds them. As a disciple of Christ, we need to cultivate a love for discipline. The Word of God corrects us every time we pick it up. Yes, it is difficult to hear where we are falling short, but we should never be offended by correction, even if it is coming from a human representative of God. For some who have years on them, they may believe that with gray hair, they are wise from life experience. Even so, the Bible is filled with knowledge, understanding, and wisdom, from God, who has no beginning, and we will never live long enough, that we do not need counsel from time to time.

How Is God Outside of or Beyond Time?

God and the Angels Live In the Spiritual Heavens Outside of or Beyond Time and Physical Creation

Edward D. Andrews

Satan Cast Out of Heaven

Revelation 12:7-9, 12 Updated American Standard Version (UASV)

⁷ And war broke out in heaven: Michael and his angels made war with the dragon, and the dragon and its angels waged war, ⁸ but they were not strong enough, nor was a place found for them any longer in heaven. ⁹ And the great dragon was thrown down, the serpent of old who is called the devil and Satan, who deceives the whole inhabited earth; he was thrown down to the earth, and his angels were thrown down with him. ¹² Therefore, rejoice, O heavens and you who dwell in them! Woe to you, O earth and sea, for the devil has come down to you in great wrath, because he knows he has a short time."

We see that the Greek term for **heaven** (*ouranos*) has been used three times here in Revelation 12:7-9, 12. What and where is this heaven that Satan is fighting a war in before he and his demon angels were cast out by Michael the archangel and his angels. First, let us make a clear statement about God, the Creator of the heavens and the earth, he has existed for all time, and he was alone before creation had a beginning.—Psalm 90:1-2; 1 Timothy 1:17.

How Many Heavens?

The Hebrew *shamayim*, which is rendered **heaven(s)** is always in the plural has the sense of the abode (dwelling place) of God and the angels, carrying the idea of that which is of great heights or towering. (Ps 103:11; Pr 25:3; Isa 55:9) The Greek word for heaven (ouranos, singular) also has the basic sense the abode (dwelling place) of God and the angels.

The Physical Heavens

The original language terms of both Hebrew and Greek express all that encompasses the physical **heavens**. The interpreter will have to look at the context to determine just what aspect of the physical heavens is meant.

The Earth's Atmosphere

The **heaven(s)** can apply to the full extent of the earth's atmosphere, which would include the dew of heaven and the frost of heaven Genesis 27:28; Job 38:29), the winged bird that flies in the air, literally heavens (Deuteronomy 4:17; Proverbs 30:19; Matthew 6:26), the winds blow in the heavens (Ps 78:26), lightning flashes from under the sky, literally heaven (Lu 17:24), and the clouds and dark clouds drop their rain, snow, or hailstones (Joshua 10:11; 1 Kings 18:45; Isaiah 55:10; Acts 14:17). "The sky" is sometimes meant as the region above the earth beyond where the birds fly to the stars, what looks like a dome that surrounds the earth.—Matthew 16:1-3; Acts 1:10-11.

Outer Space

The physical heavens that are beyond the earth's atmosphere that encompasses our solar system, galaxy, and universe(s), is referred to as **the army of the heavens** (the host of heaven, ESV, CSB, LEB, NASB), which include the sun and the moon and the stars. Genesis 1:1 outer space before the earth was developed to the point where humans could inhabit it.

In Midheaven

This expression applies to that part of the earth's atmosphere where the birds fly, such as the eagle. At the zenith or extremities of the sky.—Revelation 8:13; 14:6; 19:17; Deuteronomy 4:11.

Heavens of the Heavens

This refers to the all of our physical heavens in all directions from the earth, the billions of universes. – Deuteronomy 10:14; Nehemiah 9:6.

The Spiritual Heavens

This is the abode, the dwelling place of God and the angels, which is outside of all the physical universes. (Jude 6; Genesis 28:12, 13; Matthew 18:10; 24:36) These heavens are the "house" Jesus referred to when he said: "In my Father's house are many dwelling places [or many obodes]; but if not, I would have told you; for I go to prepare a place for you." (John 14:2) In these heavens we find, the Father, the Son, the Holy Spirit, the Seraphs, the Cherubs, the angels, and now those humans who have been resurrected to heavenly life. (See Revelation chapter 12; Daniel 7:10) What do these heavens look like, what are they like? The Bible does not state this for a very good reason, as it is highly unlikely that we can comprehend such a place. It would be foolish on our part to speculate, as the apostle Paul tells us that "flesh and blood cannot inherit the kingdom of God."—1 Corinthians 15:50.

Just as the physical heavens of the universes are far removed from the earth, so too are the heavens of God's abode or dwelling place, God's throne. Jesus said, "See that you do not despise one of these little ones. For I tell you that in heaven their **angels always see the face of my Father who is in heaven.**" This implies that not all angels at all times have access to the presence of the Father. We read, "Thus says theLord: "Heaven is my throne." The apostle Paul tells us, "For Christ did not enter a holy place made with hands, a mere copy of the true one, but into heaven itself, now to appear in the presence of God for us."—Matthew 18:10; Isaiah 66:1; Hebrews 9:24.

Outside of Time or Beyond Time

It should be noted again that the Creator of the heavens and the earth, he has existed for all time, and he was alone before creation had a beginning, he is eternal, that is timeless in both directions of what we know as time. For the Christian, God created the universes and all things physical, but for the reasonable and rational atheist scientist, the First Cause is the belief that the universes had a beginning and that before that beginning, something had to have existed that was without beginning, that extended back indefinitely. So, for the Christian side, they **presuppose** *someone eternal* **created** the universes, while the scientists **presuppose** *something eternal* **caused** the universes to come into existence. After one has taken the time to consider the minuscule that science has uncovered about the design of our universes and humans, we must ask which alternative seems more reasonable. intelligent design means an intelligent designer.

Not only do the luminaries offer us signs of God's existence, but they were specifically created for the purpose of marking accurately the natural seasons, days, and years. (Genesis 1:14-18; Psalm 74:16; 148:3) Given that both Christians and science agree that the universes came into existence, the only reasonable, rational view of time is that it too had a beginning and came into existence. The eternity of God or the First Cause before the creation of the angels, the universes and humans would not require the existence of time. In God's creation of the physical universes for the human family, he also created time for the sake of his relationship with man and man's co-existence with God. Thus, it is reasonable to suppose that God was timeless before his creative activity when he was alone.

This refers to the all of our physical heavens in all directions from the earth, the billions of universes. – Deuteronomy 10:14; Nehemiah 9:6.

Praying Unto God

R. A. Torrey

We have seen something of the tremendous importance and the resistless power of prayer, and now we come directly to the question—how to pray with power.

1. In the 12th chapter of the Acts of the Apostles, we have the record of a prayer that prevailed with God and brought to pass great results. In the 5th verse of this chapter, the manner and method of this prayer are described in few words:

"Prayer was made without ceasing of the church *unto God* for him."

The first thing to notice in this verse is the brief expression "unto God." The prayer that has power is the prayer that is offered unto God.

But some will say, "Is not all prayer unto God?"

No. Very much of so-called prayer, both public and private, is not unto God. In order that a prayer should be really unto God, there must be a definite and conscious approach to God when we pray; we must have a definite and vivid realization that God is bending over us and listening as we pray. In very much of our prayer there is really but little thought of God. Our mind is taken up with the thought of what we need and is not occupied with the thought of the mighty and loving Father of whom we are seeking it. Oftentimes it is the case that we are occupied neither with the need nor with the One to whom we are praying, but our mind is wandering here and there throughout the world. There is no power in that sort of prayer. But when we really come into God's presence, really meet Him face to face in the place of prayer, really seek the things that we desire *from Him,* then there is power.

If then, we would pray aright, the first thing that we should do is to see to it that we really get an audience with God, that we really get into His very presence. Before a word of petition is offered, we should have the definite and vivid consciousness that we are talking to God and should believe that He is listening to our petition and is going to grant the thing that we ask of Him. This is only possible by the Holy Spirit's power, so we should look to the Holy Spirit to really lead us into the presence of God, and should not be hasty in words until He has actually brought us there.

One night a very active Christian man dropped into a little prayer-meeting that I was leading. Before we knelt to pray, I said something like the above, telling all the friends to be sure before they prayed, and while they were praying, that they really were in God's presence, that they had the thought of Him definitely in mind, and to be more taken up with Him than with their petition. A few days after I met this same gentleman, and he said that this simple thought was entirely new to him, that it had made prayer an entirely new experience to him.

If then we would pray aright, these two little words must sink deep into our hearts, "*unto God.*"

2. The second secret of effective praying is found in the same verse, in the words "*without ceasing.*"

In the Revised Version, "without ceasing" is rendered "earnestly." Neither rendering gives the full force of the Greek. The word means literally "stretched-out-ed-ly." It is a pictorial word, and wonderfully expressive. It represents the soul on a stretch of earnest and intense desire. "Intensely" would perhaps come as near translating it as any English word. It is the word used of our Lord in Luke 22:44 where it is said, "He prayed more earnestly: and His sweat was as it were great drops of blood falling down to the ground."

We read in Heb. 5:7 that "in the days of His flesh" Christ "offered up prayers and supplications with strong crying and tears." In Rom. 15:30, Paul beseeches the saints in Rome to *strive* together with him in their prayers. The word translated "strive" means primarily to contend as in athletic games or in a fight. In other words, the prayer that prevails with God is the prayer into which we put our whole soul, stretching out toward God in intense and agonizing desire. Much of our modern prayer has no power in it because there is no heart in it. We rush into God's presence, run through a string of petitions, jump up and go out. If someone should ask us an hour afterward for what we prayed, oftentimes we could not tell. If we put so little heart into our prayers, we cannot expect God to put much heart into answering them.

We hear much in our day of the rest of faith, but there is such a thing as the fight of faith in prayer as well as in effort. Those who would have us think that they have attained to some sublime height of faith and trust because they never know any agony of conflict or of prayer, have surely gotten beyond their Lord, and beyond the mightiest victors for God, both in effort and prayer, that the ages of Christian history have known. When we learn to come to God with an intensity of desire that wrings the soul, then shall we know a power in prayer that most of us do not know now.

But how shall we attain to this earnestness in prayer?

Not by trying to work ourselves up into it. The true method is explained in Rom. 8:26, "And in like manner the Spirit also helpeth our infirmity: for we know not how to pray as we ought; but the Spirit Himself maketh intercession for us with groanings which cannot be uttered." (R. V.) The earnestness that we work up in the energy of the flesh is a repulsive thing. The earnestness wrought in us by the power of the Holy Spirit is pleasing to God. Here again, if we would pray aright, we must look to the Spirit of God to teach us to pray.

It is in this connection that fasting comes. In Dan. 9:3 we read that Daniel set his face "unto the Lord God, to seek by prayer and supplications, with fasting, and sackcloth, and ashes." There are those who think that fasting belongs to the old dispensation; but when we look at Acts 14:23, and Acts 13:2, 3, we find that it was practiced by the earnest men of the apostolic day.

If we would pray with power, we should pray with fasting. This, of course, does not mean that we should fast every time we pray; but there are times of emergency or special crisis in work or in our individual lives, when men of downright earnestness will withdraw themselves even from the gratification of natural appetites that would be perfectly proper under other circumstances, that they may give themselves up wholly to prayer. There is a peculiar power in such a prayer. Every great crisis in life and work should be met in that way. There is nothing pleasing to God in our giving up in a purely Pharisaic and legal way things which are pleasant, but there is power in that downright earnestness and determination to obtain in prayer the things of which we sorely feel our need, that leads us to put away everything, even things in themselves most right and necessary, that we may set our faces to find God, and obtain blessings from Him.

3. The third secret of right praying is also found in this same verse, Acts 12:5. It appears in the three words "*of the church.*"

There is power in *united prayer.* Of course, there is power in the prayer of an individual, but there is vastly increased power in united prayer. God delights in the unity of His people and seeks to emphasize it in every way, and so He pronounces a special blessing upon united prayer. We read in Matt. 18:19, "If two of you shall agree on earth as touching anything that they shall ask, it shall be done for them of My Father which is in heaven." This unity, however, must be real. The passage just quoted does not say that if two shall agree in asking, but if two shall agree *as touching* anything they shall ask. Two persons might agree to ask for the same thing, and yet there be no real agreement as touching the thing they asked. One might ask it because he really desired it, the other might ask it simply to please his friend. But where there is real agreement, where the Spirit of God brings two believers into perfect harmony as concerning that which they may ask of God, where the Spirit lays the same burden on two hearts; in all such prayer, there is absolutely irresistible power.

NTTC John 5:4: Who Took John 5:4 Out of My Bible?

Edward D. Andrews

The Healing at the Pool of Bethzatha

John 5:1-9 Updated American Standard Version (UASV)

5 After these things there was a feast of the Jews, and Jesus went up to Jerusalem.

² Now there is in Jerusalem by the Sheep Gate a pool, in Hebrew called Bethsaida,[1] which has five colonnades. ³ In these lay a multitude of sick ones, blind, lame, and paralyzed. ⁴—[2] ⁵ And a certain man was there who had been in his sickness for thirty-eight years. ⁶ When Jesus saw this man lying there and knew that he had been there a long time already, he said to him, "Do you want to become well?" ⁷ The sick man answered him, "Sir, I have no one to put me into the pool when the water is stirred up, and while I am going another steps down before me." ⁸ Jesus said to him,

"Get up, pick up your cot, and walk." 9 And immediately the man became well, and he picked up his cot and walked.

[1] Bethsaida has the best documentary evidence and is the original wording ($\mathfrak{P}^{66}\mathfrak{P}^{66}$ $\mathfrak{P}^{75}$ B W[1]), the name was then changed to Bethzatha meaning "house of mercy" in א (L it^e, 33 Eusebius), which is fair manuscript support as well as being the most difficult reading; then there is Bethesda, which also means "house of mercy" in (A C Θ 078 f.^{13} Maj), which has good documentary support.

[2] The earliest and best witnesses (MSS) $\mathfrak{P}^{66}$ $\mathfrak{P}^{75}$ א A* B C* L T D W^{supp} 33 it^{d,l} Q cop[2] Vg Sy^c **do not have** John 5:3b-4 in their exemplar; Other later witnesses (MSS) A^2 C^3 L Θ Ψ 078^{vid} Maj it[2] did have: "waiting for the moving of the water. 4 For an angel of the Lord would come down at certain seasons into the pool and stirred the water. Whoever went in first after the stirring of the water was healed of whatever disease he had." This interpolation was added by later scribes to explain the sick man's answer in verses 7 where he describes 'the water being stirred up.'

It is evident that some verses of the Greek New Testament manuscripts found in the older translations, such as the King James Version, were actually additions that were made by later copyists and were never part of the original Greek New Testament manuscripts. Matthew 17:21; 18:11; 23:14; Mark 7:16; 9:44, 46; 11:26; 15:28; Luke 17:36; 23:17; **John 5:3b, 4**; Acts 8:37; 15:34; 24:7; 28:29; and Romans 16:24.

If you read closely in John 5:1-9 in the above Updated American Standard Version, you will notice that verse 4 is missing because the count goes 1, 2, 3, 4⸺ 5, 6, 7, 8, 9. However, the second half of verse 3 is also missing as well. Missing is a poor choice of words because what was never there cannot be missing. In other words, the interpolation is missing from this translation in the main text.

One online article by Michael S. Heiser asks, "Who took John 5:4 out of the Bible?" This is where we have taken the title for our blog article. (Crosswalk.com/Bible Study Magazine)^3

The following Bible translations have **omitted John 5:3b-4** in the main text: NKJVmg ASV RSV NRSV ESV NASBmg UASV NIV TNIV NEB REB NJB NAB NLT HCSBmg NET. The mg here means that the Bible translation has retained the interpolation in the main text but omitted it in the footnote.

The following Bible translations **have retained John 5:3b-4** in the main text: KJV NKJV ASVmg RSVmg NRSVmg ESVmg NASB UASVmg NIVmg TNIVmg NEBmg REBmg NJBmg NABmg NLTmg HCSB NETmg.

---

^{3} http://tiny.cc/ny1y0y

The mg here is the opposite, and it means that the Bible translation has omitted the interpolation in the main text but retained it in the footnote.

The 2001 English Standard Version (ESV) says in its footnote on John 5:3b-4: "Some manuscripts insert, wholly or in part …" The 2012 Lexham English Bible (LEB) says in its footnote on John 5:3b-4: "The majority of later manuscripts add the following words …" the 2017 Christian Standard Bible (CSB) says in its footnote on John 5:3b-4: "Some mss include …" The 1995 New American Standard Bible (NSSB) says in its footnote on John 5:3b-4: "Early mss do not contain the remainder of v 3, nor v 4." None of these footnotes helps the Bible reader even a little. Alone, without being qualified, they mean absolutely nothing. The best of the lot is the note in the NASB. However, what kind of early mss? Of course, the worthlessness of textual footnotes in almost all modern translations is a discussion for another day. The 2018 Updated American Standard Version (UASV)on the other hand has an informative footnote. Let's return to the question that Michael S. Heiser asks, "Who took John 5:4 out of the Bible?"

The first point to be made here is the language that one uses is important. You cannot take anything **out** that was never **there** in the first place. We are certain beyond reasonable doubt[4] that the interpolation of John 5:3b-4 was added by a later scribe and was not part of the original text. Therefore, again, we must plainly ask, how does a translation take "out" words or phrases that were never "in" in the first place? I will assume that when Michael S. Heiser asks "Who took John 5:4 out of the Bible?" he meant the King James Version Bible and other pre-1900 translations as hist article infers. But what causes the confusion is the diehard KJV readers and the even more so the radical KJVO (King James Version Only)[5] readers view the KJV as the original Bible in English. Therefore, when Michael S. Heiser asks, "Who took John 5:4 out of the Bible?" the KJV readers and KJVO readers see that as being equal to asking "Who took John 5:4 out of the original?" This may even be the case with other Bible translation readers to, such as the ESV, NASB, NIV, and others.

Michael S. Heiser also asks,

> Why would verse 4 have not been included in the original New Testament? It is not because of the angel in the story. The Bible has no problem with angels; they're all over the place, doing all sorts of things. But, like today, there was a great deal of folklore and superstition about them. The idea that an angel stirred the waters at a given time during the year was one such superstition. John

---

[4] http://tiny.cc/t01y0y
[5] http://tiny.cc/c11y0y

5:7[6] mentions the stirring of the water but does not mention the angel. It's likely that John knew of the belief about the waters of Bethesda but chose to leave it out for a specific reason. Perhaps he does not wish to endorse that an angel was stirring the water. By excluding the popular belief about the angel, John focuses his readers on the healer who was indeed present—Jesus.

Here is where Michael S. Heiser, in his article, causes the confusion, ambiguity, problem for his readers. It sounds as though he believes the words (the account about **the angel** stirring the water) at John 5:3b-4 were original in some way (maybe an oral tradition) but that John left them out to avoid superstition and to focus on Jesus. Heisler writes, "It's likely that John knew of the belief about the waters of Bethesda [being stirred by an angel] but chose to leave it out for a specific reason." How can we suggest that John had known about something that is not mentioned in the original by him or any other Gospel, nor any other NT author? It is true, however, that three Church fathers, two Latin one Greek, cited the account: Tertullian (c.155–c.222), Ambrose (4th century), John Chrysostom (c.347–c.407). Whether this was an early oral tradition that a later scribe inserted into the text is not known.

What we do know is this. In looking at the **external evidence**, the best and earliest manuscript evidence does not contain this interpolation. In looking at the **internal evidence**, the style and vocabulary are not Johannine. Why would John use κινησιν [to set in motion, to move] in verse 3b and then use ταρασσω (to agitate, trouble, as water) later in verses 4 and 7? Then, we have εμβας [stepped in], which is not the usual word for getting into the water, it is καταβαινω [to come or go down, descend, to lead down, to come down, to be let down]. There is ω δηποτε [of whatsoever KJV), whatever, no matter what], which is a unique construction that does not occur anywhere else in the Greek New Testament. As well, **νοσηματι** [disease] is a unique word that does not occur anywhere else in the Greek New Testament. **Scribal activity** suggests that it is highly unlikely that a scribe would have omitted the verse because it mentioned a seemingly odd, even superstitious action of an angel.

---

[6] http://tiny.cc/321y0y

The Bible Gives Us Answers to Questions about Life

Edward D. Andrews

The Bible gives us answers to questions about this life and the one to come, which can be found nowhere else, and offers illumination to its readers. Those who take in this lifesaving knowledge are freed from the misunderstandings of life that dominate billions of others. For instance, here is one that might come to us as a shock. We are all **Mentally Bent toward Evil**.

Psalm 51:5 Updated American Standard Version (UASV)

⁵ Look, I was brought forth in error,
  and in sin did my mother conceive me.

King David had his adultery with Bathsheba and the subsequent murder of her husband exposed, for which he accepted full responsibility. His words about the human condition give us one reason for the evil of man. He says, "I was brought forth in error." What did King David's inspired words mean? **Error:** (Heb., ʿā wōn; Gr. *anomia, paranomia*) The Hebrew word *awon* essentially relates to erring, acting illegally or wrongly. This aspect of sin refers to committing a perverseness, wrongness, lawlessness, law breaking, which can also include the rejection of the sovereignty of God. It also focuses on the liability or guilt of one's wicked, wrongful act. This error may be deliberate or accidental; either willful deviation of what is right or unknowingly making a mistake. (Lev. 4:13-35;

5:1-6, 14-19; Num. 15:22-29; Ps 19:12, 13) Of course, if it is intentional; then, the consequence is far more serious. (Num. 15:30-31) Error is in opposition to the truth, and those willfully sinning corrupt the truth, a course that only brings forth flagrant sin. (Isa 5:18-23) We can be hardened by the deceitfulness of sin. – Ex 9:27, 34-35; Heb. 3:13-15.

> David stated that his problem was a corrupt heart, saying; **surely, I was sinful at birth**. He entered this world a sinner in nature long before he became a sinner in thinking, words, and actions. In fact, this internal corruption predated his **birth**, actually beginning nine months earlier when he was **conceived** in the womb. It was at conception that the Adamic sin nature was transmitted to him. The problem with what he did, sin, arose from what he was, a sinner.[7]

What is sin? **Sin**: (Heb. *chattath*; Gr. *hamartia*) Any spoken word (Job 2:10; Ps 39:1), wrong action (Lev. 20:20; 2 Cor. 12:21) or failing to act when one should have (Num. 9:13; Jam. 4:17), in mind and heart (Prov. 21:4; Rom. 3:9-18; 2 Pet 2:12-15) that is contrary to God's personality, ways, will and purposes, standards, as set out in the Scriptures. It is also a major sin to lack faith in God, doubting in mind and heart, even subtly in our actions, that he has the ability to carry out his will and purposes. (Heb. 3:12-13, 18-19). It is commonly referred to as missing the mark of perfection.

What is a sinner? **Sinner**: (Gr. *hamartōlos*) In the Scriptures "sinners" is generally used in a more specific way, that is, referring to those willfully living in sin, practicing sin, or have a reputation of sinning.–Matt. 9:10; Mark 2:15; Luke 5:30; 7:37-39; John 9:16; Rom. 3:7; Gal. 2:15; 1 Tim. 1:15; Heb. 7:26; Jam. 4:8; 1 Pet 4:18; Jude 1:15.

David is not here casting the blame onto his mother, as God never intended mothers to conceive and give birth to children who would sin. Nevertheless, when Adam and Eve rebelled, they were expelled from the Garden of Eden, they lost their ability to pass on perfection. Therefore, every child was born missing the mark of perfection. The Hebrew term translated "sin" is *chattath;* in Greek, the word is *hamartia*. Both carry the meaning of missing the mark of perfection, namely, falling short of perfection.

The verbal forms occur in enough secular contexts to provide a basic picture of the word's meaning. In Judges 20:16 the left-handed slingers of Benjamin are said to have the skill to throw stones at targets and "not miss." In a different context, Proverbs 19:2 speaks of a man in a hurry who "misses

---

[7] Anders, Max; Lawson, Steven (2004-01-01). Holman Old Testament Commentary - Psalms: 11 (p. 266). B&H Publishing. Kindle Edition.

his way" (RSV, NEB, KJV has "sinneth"). A similar idea of not finding a goal appears in Proverbs 8:36; the concept of failure is implied.[8]

Genesis 6:5 The American Translation (AT)

⁵ When the LORD saw that the wickedness of man on the earth was great, and that the **whole bent of his thinking was** never anything but **evil**, the LORD regretted that he had ever made man on the earth.

Genesis 8:21 The American Translation (AT)

²¹ I will never again curse the soil, though the **bent of man's mind** may be **evil from his very youth**; nor ever again will I ever again destroy all life creature as I have just done.

All of us have inherited a sinful nature, meaning that we are currently unable to live up to the mark of perfection, in which we were created. In fact, Genesis 6:5 says we all suffer from, 'our whole bent of thinking, which is nothing but evil." Genesis 8:21 says that 'our mind is evil from our very youth.' Jeremiah 17:9 says that our hearts are treacherous and desperately sick." What does all of this mean? It means that prior to the fall, our natural inclination; our natural leaning was toward good. However, after the fall, our natural inclination, our natural leaning was toward bad, wicked, evil.

We should never lose sight of the fact that unrighteous desires of the flesh are not to be taken lightly. (Rom. 7:19, 20) Nevertheless, if it is our desire to have a righteous relationship with God, it will be the stronger desire. Psalm 119:165 says, "Abundant peace belongs to those loving your law, and for them there is no stumbling block." We need to cultivate our love for doing right, which will strengthen our conscience, the sense of what is right and wrong that governs somebody's thoughts and actions, urging us to do right rather than wrong. It is only through studying the Bible that we can train the conscience. Once it is trained, it will prick us like a needle in the heart, when we are thinking of doing something wrong. It will feel like a pain in our heart, sadness, nervousness, which is the voice saying, 'do not do this.' Moreover, if we ignore our voice, it will grow silent over time and will stop telling us what is wrong. – Romans 2:14-15.

James 1:14-15 Updated American Standard Version (UASV)

¹⁴ But each one is tempted when he is carried away and enticed by his own desire.[9] ¹⁵ Then the desire when it has conceived gives birth to sin, and sin when it is fully grown brings forth death.

---

[8] G. Herbert Livingston, "638 חטא," ed. R. Laird Harris, Gleason L. Archer Jr., and Bruce K. Waltke, *Theological Wordbook of the Old Testament* (Chicago: Moody Press, 1999), 277.
[9] Or "own *lust*"

We have a natural desire toward wrongdoing, and Satan is the god of this world (2 Cor. 4:3-4), and he caters to the fallen flesh. James also tells us "each one is tempted when he is carried away and enticed by his own desire.[10] Then the desire when it has conceived gives birth to sin, and sin when it is fully grown brings forth death." (James 1:14-15) We resist the devil by immediately dismissing any thought that is contrary to God's values found in his Word. When any wrong thought enters our mind, we do not entertain it for a moment, nor do we cultivate it, causing it to grow. We then offer rational prayers in our head, or better yet, out loud so we can defeat irrational fleshly thinking with rational biblical thinking. The Apostle Peter, referring to the Devil wrote, "Resist him, firm in your faith, knowing that the same kinds of suffering are being experienced by your brotherhood throughout the world." (1 Pet. 5:9) While the Bible helps us better to understand the gravity of our fallen condition, this should not cause us alarm as the Bible also shows us how to control our mental bent toward evil. We can renew our mind (Rom 12:2), acquire the mind of Christ (1 Cor. 2:16)), take off the old person and put on the new person (Eph. 4:20-24; Col 3:9-10), among other things.

---

[10] Or "own *lust*"

Hebrews 5:14 and 12:23: Why is The Greek teleios and teleioō translated differently?

Edward D. Andrews

Darrell Conner from Facebook asks, returning to Hebrews 5:14, I have another question for you concerning **perfection** in [the book of] Hebrews, which I feel must be understood to properly translate Chapter 5, which as I said…no translation has done yet. So here is another question …: the UASV translates Hebrews 12:23: "to the general assembly and congregation of the firstborn who are enrolled in heaven, and to God, the Judge of all, and to the spirits of the righteous made perfect," and just curious as to why you would use the word "perfect?" Given the difference in meaning between the original word teleioó and how "perfect" is ordinarily used in modern culture, I would think "complete" would be better, particularly when you consider the Theme of Perfection in Hebrews.

Before answering your question, let us take a look at some original language texts and some translations.

Hebrews 5:14 Greek Text

```
            of complete/perfect (ones  but   is   the solid food
     14        τελείων               δέ  ἐστιν  ἡ   στερεὰ       ,
of the (ones  through the habit the senses
     τῶν        διὰ    τὴν   ἕξιν  τὰ  αἰσθητήρια
```

having been exercised (like a   having to distinguishing
γεγυμνασμένα   ἐχόντων   πρὸς   διάκρισιν
of good (thing   both and bad (thing
καλοῦ   τε   καὶ   κακοῦ.

Hebrews 5:14 Updated American Standard Version (UASV)

[14] But solid food belongs to the **mature**, to those who through practice have their discernment trained to distinguish between good and evil. (ESV, CSB, NASB, LEB reads similarly)

Hebrews 5:14 King James Version (KJV)

[14] But strong meat belongeth to them that are of **full age**, even those who by reason of use have their senses exercised to discern both good and evil.

Hebrews 12:23 Greek Text

to assembly and to ecclesia/congregation
23   πανηγύρει   καὶ   ἐκκλησίᾳ
of firstborn (ones having been enrolled in heavens and
πρωτοτόκων   ἀπογεγραμμένων   ἐν   ,   καὶ
to judge to God of all and to spirits of righteous (ones
κριτῇ   θεῷ   ,   καὶ   πνεύμασι   δικαίων
having been perfected/comp
τετελειωμένων,

Hebrews 12:23 Updated American Standard Version (UASV)
[23] to the general assembly and congregation of the firstborn who are enrolled in heaven, and to God, the Judge of all, and to the spirits of the righteous **made perfect**,

(ESV, CSB, NASB, LEB reads similarly)

Hebrews 12:23 King James Version (KJV)

[23] To the general assembly and church of the firstborn, which are written in heaven, and to God the Judge of all, and to the spirits of just men **made perfect**,

The above translations are KJV literal, NASB literal, LEB literalish, ESV essentially literal, and the CSB optimally literal. Therefore, we are not having to deal with a translation that has the main goal of being interpretive, namely, going beyond the Word of God.

A literal translation is a lexical translation. What does that mean? What is a lexicon? It is a technical word for a dictionary of especially the Greek,

Hebrew, Syriac, or Arabic. It gives us the English equivalents of the Greek, Hebrew, Syriac, or Arabic words. All words have more than one meaning. These meanings are the full extent of their use among the people.

The adjective **τέλειος** teleios in the lexicon can mean complete, perfect, mature. The **primary meaning** of pertaining "**to meeting the highest standard.**"

ⓐ of things, perfect

α. as acme of goodness, as adj. (ἀρετή Did., Gen. 40, 19.—Of aeons, Iren. 1, 1, 1 [Harv. I 8, 2]; Hippol., Ref. 6, 31, 4) ἔργον Js 1:4a (s. ἔργον Ib); cp. ISm 11:2. δώρημα Js 1:17 (s. δώρημα). νόμος vs. 25 (opp. the Mosaic law). ἀγάπη 1J 4:18. ἀνάλυσις 1 Cl 44:5 (Just., D. 41, 1). γνῶσις 1:2; B 1:5. πρόγνωσις 1 Cl 44:2. μνεία 56:1. ἐλπίς ISm 10:2 (v.l. πίστις); χάρις 11:1. νηστεία Hs 5, 3, 6. ναός B 4:11 (ἐκκλησία Did., Gen. 69, 14). τελειοτέρα σκηνή (s. σκηνή 2) Hb 9:11.—Subst. τὸ τέλειον what is perfect Ro 12:2.

ⓑ of persons who are fully up to standard in a certain respect and not satisfied with half-way measures perfect, complete, expert (TAM II/1, 147, 4f ἰατρὸς τέλειος

The **Second Primary** meaning is **pertaining to being mature, full-grown, mature, adult** (Aeschyl., Pla., X.+; oft. pap; Philo; Jos., Ant. 19, 362).

ⓐ adj. ἀνὴρ τέλειος Eph 4:13 (opp. νήπιοι, as Polyb. 5, 29, 2; Philo, Leg. All. 1, 94, Sobr. 9 νήπιον παιδίον πρὸς ἄνδρα τέλειον=an immature child compared to a mature man, Somn. 2, 10). In dazzling wordplay: μὴ παιδία γίνεσθε ταῖς φρεσίν, ἀλλὰ τῇ κακίᾳ νηπιάζετε, ταῖς δὲ φρεσὶν τέλειοι γίνεσθε do not think like children, yet do be infants as respects evil, while at the same time grown-up in your thinking 1 Cor 14:20.

ⓑ subst. (Dio Chrys. 34 [51], 8 οἱ τ.; Diogenes, Ep. 31, 3 οἱ τ. … οἱ παῖδες; Ath., R. 17 p. 68, 31) τελείων ἐστὶν ἡ στερεὰ τροφή solid food is (only) for adults Hb 5:14 (opp. νήπιος).

The **third primary** meaning is "**pertaining to being a cult initiate, initiated.**" ()

The **fourth primary** meaning is pertaining "**to being fully developed in a moral sense.**"

ⓐ of humans **perfect, fully developed** (Hippol., Ref. 1, 19, 16) in a moral sense τέλειος ἀνήρ Js 3:2 (s. RHöistad, ConNeot 9, '44, p. 22f). τὸν τέλειον ἄνθρωπον GMary 463, 26f (restored). Mostly without a noun εἰ θέλεις τέλειος εἶναι Mt 19:21 (EYarnold, TU 102, '68, 269–73). Cp. I Eph 15:2; D 1:4; 6:2. Pl. Mt 5:48a; ISm 11:3a. W. ὁλόκληροι Js 1:4b. W. πεπληροφορημένοι Col 4:12.

ⓑ of God **perfect** (Pind., Aeschyl. et al.; Theocr., Diod S, Plut. et al.; Tat.4, 2, 12; 4, 15, 2; Theoph. Ant. 2, 15 [p. 138, 12]) Mt 5:48b (i.e. God is a role model for unlimited display of beneficence; cp. on this verse Hierocles 18 p. 459: the goal is τὴν πρὸς θεὸν ὁμοίωσιν κτήσασθαι 'attainment of likeness to God.'—William Arndt et al., A Greek-English Lexicon of the New Testament and Other Early Christian Literature (Chicago: University of Chicago Press, 2000), 995-996.

The verb **τελειόω teleioō** in the lexicon can mean completeness, perfection, maturity. There are three main different meanings for this Greek verb in the vocabulary use of the first-century Greek-speaking people, one of which has several different senses. The **primary** meaning is "to complete an activity, complete, bring to an end, finish, accomplish." Perfect comes into play in that it is a synonym of complete because something that is complete is perfect, something that is perfect is complete. (Heb. 7:19; 11:40) The **secondary meaning** is "to overcome or supplant an imperfect state of things by one that is free from objection, bring to an end, bring to its goal/accomplishment."

ⓐ of Jesus ἔπρεπεν αὐτῷ (i.e. τῷ θεῷ) διὰ παθημάτων τελειῶσαι (Ἰησοῦν) Hb 2:10 (i.e., as the context indicates, he receives highest honors via suffering and death in his identification w. humanity); pass., 5:9; 7:28. This is usu. understood to mean the **completion** and **perfection** of Jesus by the overcoming of earthly limitations (s. Windisch, Hdb. exc. on Hb 5:9.

ⓑ **bring to full measure, fill the measure of** τὶ something. τὰς ἀποκαλύψεις καὶ τὰ ὀράματα Hv 4, 1, 3. ἐτελείωσαν κατὰ τῆς κεφαλῆς αὐτῶν τὰ ἁμαρτήματα GPt 5:17 (κατά A 2bγ).

ⓒ **fulfill** of prophecies, promises, etc., which arouse expectation of events or happenings that correspond to their wording (τελείωσις 2.—Jos., Ant. 15, 4 θεοῦ τοὺς λόγους τελειώσαντος; Artem. 4, 47 p. 228, 19 ἐλπίδας) ἡ πίστις πάντα ἐπαγγέλλεται, πάντα τελειοῖ Hm 9:10; pass. be fulfilled ἐξαίφνης τελειωθήσεται τὸ βούλημα αὐτοῦ 1 Cl 23:5.—MPol 16:2ab. The promises of the prophets find their fulfillment, by implication, in the gospel ISm 7:2. This may be the place for J 19:28 (so Bultmann.—S. 1 above).
ⓓ of the perfection of upright pers. who have gone on before, pass. (Wsd 4:13; Philo, Leg. All. 3, 74 ὅταν τελειωθῇς καὶ βραβείων καὶ στεφάνων ἀξιωθῇς) πνεύματα δικαίων τετελειωμένων Hb 12:23. So perh. also 11:40 and Lk 13:32 (s. 1 above).
ⓔ **make perfect**

α. someone ὁ νόμος οὐδέποτε δύναται τοὺς προσερχομένους τελειῶσαι Hb 10:1; likew. perh. (s. 1 above) 7:19 (then οὐδέν would refer to humanity). κατὰ συνείδησιν τελειῶσαι τὸν λατρεύοντα 9:9. Perh. 10:14 (s. 3 below). Pass. in act. sense become perfect (Zosimus: Hermet. IV p. 111, 15f

28

) D 16:2; ἔν τινι in something. (Jos., Ant. 16, 6) ἐν (τῇ) ἀγάπῃ 1J 4:18; 1 Cl 49:5; 50:3. W. inf. foll. B 6:19. ἵνα ὦσιν τετελειωμένοι εἰς ἕν in order that they might attain perfect unity J 17:23.—Also in an unfavorable sense τελειωθῆναι τοῖς ἁμαρτήμασιν B 14:5.—For Phil 3:12 s. 3 below. β. someth. The Lord is called upon, in the interest of his community τελειῶσαι αὐτὴν ἐν τῇ ἀγάπῃ σου D 10:5. Pass. (Philo, Somn. 1, 131 ψυχὴ τελειωθεῖσα ἐν ἄθλοις ἀρετῶν) ἐκ τῶν ἔργων ἡ πίστις ἐτελειώθη faith was perfected in good deeds Js 2:22. Of love 1J 2:5; 4:12, 17. Cp. 2 Cor 12:9 v.l.

The **third primary meaning** is As a term of mystery religions **consecrate, initiate,** pass. be consecrated, become a τέλειος (s. τέλειος 3) Phil 3:12 (though mng. 2eα is also prob.). Some of the Hb-passages (s. 2a; eα above) may belong here, esp. those in which a consecration of Jesus is mentioned 2:10; 5:9; 7:28 (s. THaering, Monatschr. für Pastoraltheol. 17, 1921, 264–75.—William Arndt et al., A Greek-English Lexicon of the New Testament and Other Early Christian Literature (Chicago: University of Chicago Press, 2000), 996.

The above is just one translation tool of many that are used. Any of the meanings are considered a literal translation. The choice of which word or phrase that you use is based on the context. The meaning of a word or an expression may change depending on the context in which it is used. It is important that you have concord (rendering the same word the same in each occurrence) but good judgment must be used because this translation philosophy is not an absolute. Literal Translators must seek to use the same rendering every time it is acceptable and the context does not require otherwise.

of complete/perfect (ones but is the solid food
14   τελείων   δέ ἐστιν ἡ στερεὰ   ,

Literally, the solid food is but (only) for adults. The context here in Hebrews 5:13-14 suggests that τέλειοι has the meaning "mature, adult." The maturity here is spiritual. This is one of our three potential lexical definitions.

of righteous (ones
23   δικαίων
having been perfected/comp
τετελειωμένων,

Literally, righteous ones have been perfected, made perfect, completed. The context here is that in the end, the ones having a righteous standing before God will be made perfect. In the end, Christ will bring these ones to the goal of perfection. The lexical meaning available to the translator is completeness, perfection, maturity.

While I have said that one should not translate with their theological lenses on, this does not mean that we do not interpret what the author meant by the words that they used. It is vitally important that we get at what the author means in Bible translation; otherwise, we could not find the context to determine which of our lexical choices fit. The thing is we want to fit our lexical choices to the meaning of the original language words, giving us our English equivalent. But we do not want to take our theological views so much into consideration that they are guiding our choices. It isn't just the Updated American Standard Version that rendered teleioō as **made perfect**. This is the case of all of the literal and semi-literal translations. It fits the context best.

THE ATHEIST: Mistaken Views of Christianity, the Bible, and God

Edward D. Andrews

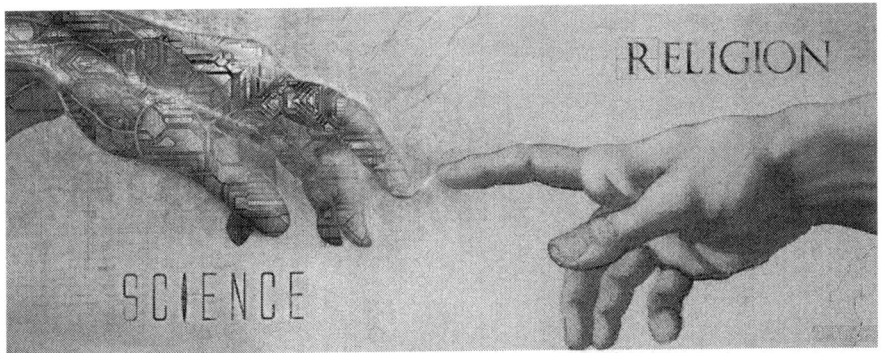

Atheists make some valid points about the difficulty that Christians and Christianity find themselves in today. However, it is more complex than what they believe to be true. The reason atheism is booming (if we could even use that term with such a small amount), is because of biblical illiteracy within Christianity. Christianity is 90% biblically illiterate. These ones are barely able to explain their doctrinal positions let alone defend the faith. Moreover, atheists are more apologetic and evangelistic about their beliefs. In addition, atheists tend to read more atheistic apologetic books that supposedly undermine Christianity, the Bible, and God. Christians are just now finding their way into Christian apologetics.

The last 40-50 years have seen many Christian leaders taking on Christian apologetics and Christian Philosophy being of serious interest. The irony is, if an atheist, who is well read comes across dozens of biblically illiterate Christians online, they believe that Christianity, the Bible, and God are indefensible. However, this is not the case because if they were to encounter a William Lane Craig, Norm Geisler, Ravi Zacharias, John Lennox, Gary Habermas, Hugh Ross, or any one of the hundreds of other Christian apologists, it would be a completely different outcome.

What many fails to understand is, Christianity being attacked by the so-called intellectuals of the world is nothing new, it has gone on for 2,000 years. Think about this, in 33 C.E.[11] there were 120 Christians in a world of

---

[11] B.C.E. means "before the Common Era," which is more accurate than B.C. ("before Christ"). C.E. denotes "Common Era," often called A.D., for *anno Domini*, meaning "in the year of our Lord."

Greek Philosophy. Within 120 years, the number of Christians grew to over a million out of a one hundred million population. However, this was also the era that began the fragmentation of Christianity too. Will Durant states: "Celsus [second-century opponent of Christianity] himself had sarcastically observed that Christians were 'split up into ever so many factions, each individual desiring to have his own party.' About 187 [C.E.] Irenaeus listed twenty varieties of Christianity; about 384 [C.E.] Epiphanius counted eighty."—The Story of Civilization: Part III—Caesar and Christ.

Today there are over 41,000 different varieties of Christianity, all divided against one another, all believing different from one another, all being vastly biblically illiterate. One might think this only spells the demise of Christianity. However, Jesus and the other New Testament authors all spoke of the great apostasy that was coming, which would fragment the Christian faith founded by Christ and grown by the apostles. They spoke of true Christianity and false Christianity, and that both would grow together but that false Christianity would outgrow true Christianity. This has come true exactly as it was described in great detail 2,000 years ago. On the horizon is a great harvest that is to come where there will be a reckoning for those Christians who believed that they were doing the right thing but like the atheist and agnostic, they are very much mistaken.

Matthew 7:21-23 Updated American Standard Version (UASV)

[21] "**Not everyone** [i.e., not every Christian] who says to me, 'Lord, Lord,' will enter the kingdom of heaven, but **the one who does the will of my Father** who is in heaven. [22] On that day **many will say** to me, 'Lord, Lord, did we not prophesy in your name, and cast out demons in your name, and do many mighty works in your name?' [23] And then **I will declare to them**, 'I never knew you; depart from me, you who practice lawlessness.'

- Not every Christian will be found to have a righteous standing before God at Jesus second coming

- Only those doing the will of the Father will have a righteous standing

- Thus, the question that begs to be answered is, "what is the will of the Father according to God's Word not our subjective opinion?'

- The vast majority of Christians and Christianity believe that they are the truth and the way today and that they are doing the will of the Father

- However, to these ones, Jesus will say, 'I never knew you; depart from me, you who practice lawlessness.'

There is the mistaken view that true Christians want to save the whole of humankind. This is not true; they are not interested in those unbelievers with unreceptive hearts. They are not interested in those unbelievers with closed minds. They are not interested in false Christians who are blinded by their theological biases. The evangelistic objective is that true Christians save some but that they evangelize all. Right now, true Christianity is getting its footing back and is growing defenders of the faith. THE CULTURE WAR: How the West Lost Its Greatness & Was Weakened From Within by Hanne Nabintu Herland is a part of that wakeup call. Christian Publishing House and thousands of Christian apologists around the world are building an army of Christian defenders of the faith, of God's Word, and of God Himself.

YOUTH: Is There Anything Wrong with Flirting

Edward D. Andrews

Flirting is behaving in a playfully alluring way through words or actions that you are romantically interested in a person of the opposite sex. Is it wrong for you to show another that you are romantically interested in them? Not really, like most things, it all depends on your intentions. If you are interested in another romantically, it makes sense that you have to make your intentions known, if you are going to know if they feel the same.

However, flirting just when you have no romantic intentions toward another would be wrong. There are popular young persons in your school, who get most of the attention. However, even they have that someone that they are attracted too, secretly wishing the feeling were mutual. How would this popular person, who, on the surface, seems to get everything he or she wants, feel if that other person flirted with them, getting their hopes up, and they are not really interested all? It is fine to give someone special attention because you do want a romantic relationship. However, it only causes pain and hurt to toy with someone's feelings, leading him or her on, and then pull the rug out from under him or her because you were never serious.

Why do some people flirt with others when they have no romantic intentions? Some are only concerned with their own exaggerated sense of self-importance. These ones know that everyone is interested in them, which causes a power trip where they crave the attention. This is an act of callous disregard for the other person's feelings. The empty-headed like to treat life and others as their plaything. You should seek to do what is right.

The Dangers of Flirting

Flirting will ruin their reputation in the end. Yes, there is an immediate satisfaction from their crowd of friends. However, in the end, it will catch up with them because treating others like crap for entertainment will only be funny for a very select heartless few. If the person flirting for entertainment, having no real interest, continues down this path, he or she will discover that ninety-nine percent of the school will see them as disgusting. Love cares more for others than for self. Love doesn't want what it doesn't really want. Love doesn't walk around arrogantly looking for attention; it isn't full of themselves, it doesn't show flirtatious interest on others with no intentions, it is not always thinking of itself.

Flirting will hurt the person you flirt with. There is not one young person who would ever want to be flirted with by a person, who is just seeking attention for himself or herself. Almost none would want to be around a person, who is flirty. They know that the only reason the flirt is even speaking to them is that it is a game. You see, in the end, no one takes a flirt serious because he or she could never really know his or her true intentions. Once a person has a reputation as a flirt, it is very difficult to undo. Try to do what is good for others, not just what is good for you. Think, have you ever thought for even a moment that someone was romantically interested in you? Then, you discover that you were wrong. The feeling is very painful and if things like this happen enough, it can lead to your not being able to trust anyone.

Flirting will destroy any hope of having genuine romance. Who would want to marry a person that has the reputation of being a flirt? Who would want to date a person that has a reputation as a flirt? How could you ever trust a flirt? He or she is seen talking one on one with someone of the opposite sex, the first thing in your mind is, complete suspicion that he or she is flirting. Moreover, how could you ever know if he or she truly loved you? You should never spend time with people who lie. You should never keep company with pretenders. Let me add a note to these last two thoughts. All of us have lied. Some of us have lied because it seemed like the right thing to do to avoid embarrassment or something that would hurt another. All of us have pretended in a relationship; try to be the best person we can. On a small scale, these are harmless to a degree. It is when a person is a malicious liar, having a desire to cause harm or pain to another for recreational purposes or even evil intentions. Flirts are not attractive people.

When a person flirts, they hurt people, who then tell others what type of person you are. The more you flirt, the further the word will spread, until one day; you have no one to flirt with, and no one to date romantically. If you do not stop with the flirting, you might as well prepare yourself for a lonely life of isolation.

"Flirting reveals the wishful intent of the heart and when it has no romantic intentions then it is nothing more than manipulation."–Terry.

1 Corinthians 13:4-5 Updated American Standard Version (UASV)

⁴ Love is long suffering and kind; Love is not jealous, it does not brag; it is not puffed up,[12] ⁵ does not behave indecently;[13] is not seeking its own interests, is not provoked, does not keep a record of wrong,

1 Corinthians 10:24 Updated American Standard Version (UASV)

²⁴ Let each one keep seeking, not his own good, but that of the other person.

Psalm 26:4 Updated American Standard Version (UASV)

⁴ I do not sit with men of falsehood,
nor do I go about with hypocrites.

---

[12] I.e., self-important or made proud
[13] Or *is not rude*

What Is Doubt

Edward D. Andrews

Below is a section that has been taken from *The Baker Encyclopedia of Psychology and Counseling*, Second Edition, which will help our readers better understand what doubt is and when it has become a problem to the point of being concerned.

Doubt. A state of mind characterized by an absence of either assent or dissent to a certain proposition. It is a suspension of commitment to belief or disbelief, either because the evidence pro and con is evenly balanced (positive doubt) or because evidence is lacking for either side (negative doubt, exemplified by the apostle Thomas). Doubt is thus an integral part of each person's belief system, since it is impossible for anyone to believe or disbelieve with complete certainty all propositions of which he or she is aware. Yet in spite of the natural occurrence of doubt in human cognition, many people view doubt as a negative mindset to be avoided if at all possible.

Doubt is a topic of interest to scholars from three academic disciplines. Philosophers study doubt because of its epistemological implications in relation to knowledge, truth, and awareness of existence. Theologians are concerned with doubt because it often occurs as a prelude to belief or as a precursor of disbelief. Psychologists investigate doubt because of the emotions that often accompany it (anxiety, depression, or fear) and because in certain pathologies doubt can become obsessional and debilitating.

Doubt, Unbelief, and Ambivalence. One can differentiate between doubt and unbelief. Unbelief is a positive conviction of falsity regarding an issue and hence is a form of belief. Doubt does not imply a belief in a contrary position; it is simply being unconvinced. If, however, doubt becomes pervasive and dominates the thinking of a person regarding all issues, it is more appropriately called skepticism or definitive doubt. The skeptic despairs of ever knowing truth with certainty.

One can also distinguish doubt from ambivalence. Ambivalence is a state of mind characterized by the concurrent presence of two or more differing feelings toward the same object. Indecisiveness and vacillation, although related to doubt, refer more to a lack of commitment to a proposition or to a frequent change of opinion. Ambivalence in massive quantities is classically seen as a primary indicator of schizophrenia, whereas massive doubt is more often a part of obsessional disorders.

One can differentiate between normal doubt and abnormal doubt chiefly by the degree to which the doubt impairs daily living. Doubt is normal when it does not dominate a person's thinking, when it is overshadowed by stable beliefs, and when the goal of the doubt is resolution into belief or disbelief. Doubt is also normal when employed, as René Descartes advocated, for the purpose of seeking truth. Normal doubt is a type of mental clarification and can help a person better organize his or her beliefs. Developmental theorists have noted several phases of life when doubts are characteristically found: in adolescence, when the teenager moves from childhood credulity toward a personalized belief system, and in the middle years, when issues of competence and direction predominate (Grant, 1974). Abnormal doubt, unlike normal doubt, focuses on issues having little consequence or issues without grave implications of error.

Religious Doubt. Religious doubt has been a concern of believers from biblical days to the present. In the garden of Eden the serpent used doubt as a tool to move Eve from a position of belief to one of disobedience. Abraham, Job, and David all had times of doubt that were painful yet growth-producing. The best-known example of doubt in the Bible is Thomas, who was absent when Jesus made a post resurrection appearance to the ten apostles. Jesus showed the ten his hands and his side (John 20), evidence that dispelled their doubt as to his identity. When told of Jesus' appearance, Thomas replied that he would not believe until he too had seen the evidence. Eight days later Jesus reappeared, showed Thomas his wounds, and made a gracious plea for faith.

By way of contrast, Jesus consistently condemned unbelief wherever he found it. Jesus presumably tolerated doubt because it was a transitory, nonpermanent state of mind, whereas he condemned unbelief because it was a fixed decision often accompanied by hardness of heart. Guinness (1976) cautions, however, that Scripture sometimes uses the word *unbelief* to refer to doubt (Mark 9:24). Hence exegetical care is needed when interpreting the Bible's teachings regarding doubt.

Doubt is a problem in theological systems committed to inscripturated truth. For example, evangelical Christians are generally not tolerant of doubt if it is prolonged, unyielding, and centered on cardinal truths. Doubt is not so much a problem in liberal theologies since truth in those systems is more relative and less certain. Thus the conservative Christian community sees doubt as risky and dangerous, whereas the liberal Christian community sees doubt as a sign of healthy intellectual inquiry. Some psychologists of religion even see doubt, particularly as envisioned within a questing religious orientation (see Batson, Schoenrade, & Ventis, 1993), as an indication of religious maturity.

Normal doubt tends to appear when a person's belief system "does not protect the individual in his life experiences and from its more painful states" (Halfaer, 1972, p. 216). Doubt is resolved into belief or disbelief in any of four ways: through conversion, through liberalization, through renewal, or through emotional growth. Individuals can construct rigid defenses designed to ensure belief and prevent doubt at all costs such as sometimes occurs in cults that discourage any reexamination of beliefs. (Benner and Hill 1985, 1999, P. 368)

In short, doubt as it relates to God or his Word is when we feel unconvinced or uncertain about some biblical teaching or some trustworthy aspect of God's Word. Someone might say, "I feel, I think, or I believe that the Bible is unlikely to be completely without error." Some may have a feeling or state of uncertainty, especially as to whether a certain biblical position on a particular teaching is true, or as to whether the Word of God as a whole is accurate or trustworthy. Some may feel that it is unlikely that the Bible is one hundred present true, or beneficial for the world we live in today.

Divisions In the Church

There are 41,000 different denominations, each of which teaches different views on the various Bible doctrines, such as salvation, sanctification, eternal security, the charismatic gifts, women in the ministry, the length of the Genesis creation days, the human constitution (Christian anthropology), and the like. Each Bible doctrine has, at least, two different views, with some having four or more. Therefore, not all of the various views of a particular doctrine can be true. For example, under the human constitution or Christian anthropology, there are three views: Two parts (Dichotomism), Three parts (Trichotomism), and One part (Monism).

The traditional position of many theologians in some denominations is the **Dichotomist view**, which believes that the human being is formed of two components: material (body/flesh) and spiritual (soul/spirit). The **Trichotomist** believes that human beings are made up of three distinct components: body or flesh, soul, and spirit. A significant minority of theologians in some denominations holds this view. The **Monist** believes that the body and soul are **not** considered separate components of a person, but rather as two facets of a united whole. Modern theologians more and more are taking this position, as well as modern neuroscience. Now, the point being, not all three views can be correct. Thus, not all doubts are necessarily a bad thing. Let us suppose that one of these is the absolute truth and we hold one of the other two positions. After much research, our conclusion based on previous knowledge is revised, so that we now take the position that is absolutely true, meaning that the doubts about our former position were warranted.

A recently new belief among liberal and some moderate Bible scholars is relativism. Relativism is the belief that concepts such as right and wrong, goodness and badness, or truth and falsehood are not absolute but change from culture to culture and situation to situation, even person to person. Thus, as silly as it might sound, a relativist would argue that all three of the above positions on the human constitution would be true for different people that hold those positions. Episcopal Bishop John Shelby Spong (liberal theologian) commented: "We must ... move from thinking we have the truth and others must come to our point of view to the realization that ultimate truth is beyond the grasp of all of us."[14] As conservative Christians, we hold that there is absolute truth. Jesus said, "You will know the truth, and the truth will set you free." (John 8:32) The apostle Paul wrote, "This is good, and it is acceptable in the sight of God our Savior, who desires all

---

[14] But Mr. Myers...! | Uncommon Descent, http://tiny.cc/xar64x (accessed October 26, 2015).

men to be saved and to come to an accurate knowledge[15] of truth." (1 Tim. 2:3-4) Jesus also said, "True worshipers will worship the Father in spirit and truth, for the Father is seeking such people to worship him. God is spirit, and those who worship him must worship in spirit and truth." (John 4:23-24) Therefore, true Christians believe that absolute truth exists. As it relates to God's Word, we must carry out an exegetical investigation, to discover it.

There are a large number of books on biblical interpretation, with different rules and principles for interpreting the Scriptures, which is one reason as to why there are so many different views on a given Bible doctrine. Other reasons for different views of the same doctrine would be church tradition, lack of knowledge or interpretative skills, theological bias, and human imperfection, among other things. However, just as was true of liberal scholarship and their relativistic belief that there is no such thing as absolute truth when we know otherwise, so it is the liberal and moderate Bible scholars who use a method of interpretation that contributes to subjective interpretation, i.e., the historical-critical method. Conservative scholarship uses the objective form of interpretation, namely, the Historical-grammatical interpretation. Thus, we can see how Christians might struggle with what is the correct way to interpret Scripture. In addition, they are overwhelmed with what is the correct view of each of our Bible doctrines.

In his forward to R. C. Sproul's *Knowing Scripture*, J. I. Packer observes that Protestant theologians are in conflict about biblical interpretation. To illustrate the diversity of biblical interpretations, William Yarchin pictures a shelf full of religious books saying different things, but all claiming to be faithful interpretations of the Bible. Bernard Ramm observed that such diverse interpretations underlie the "doctrinal variations in Christendom." A mid-19th-century book on biblical interpretation observed that even those who believe the Bible to be "the word of God" hold "the most discordant views" about fundamental doctrines."[16]

Below are just a few examples of the "discordant views," i.e., conflicting views of different Bible doctrines.

Four Views of Hell	Four Views of Salvation	Two Views of Inspiration	Three Views of Atonement

---

[15] *Epignosis* is a strengthened or intensified form of *gnosis* (*epi*, meaning "additional"), meaning, "true," "real," "full," "complete" or "accurate," depending upon the context. Paul and Peter alone use *epignosis*.

[16] Biblical hermeneutics - Wikipedia, the free encyclopedia, https://en.m.wikipedia.org/wiki/Biblical_hermeneutics (accessed October 26, 2015).

Four Views of creation	Four Views of Eternal Security	Four Views of Inspiration	Four Views of Works in Final Judgment
Four Views of Inerrancy	Four Views of Sanctification	Two Views of Fasting	Four Views of the Book of Revelation
Two Views of Christology	Three Views of Image of God	Three Views of Grace	Three Views of Human Constitution
Four Views of Providence	Two Views of Lord's Supper	Four Views of Free Will	Two Views of Charismatic Gifts
Two Views of Baptism	Three Views of Jesus' Return	Two Views of Sabbath	Four Views of Predestination
Three Views of Purgatory	Four Views of the Church	Four Views of End Times	Four Views of Christian Spirituality
Four Views of Antichrist	Three Views of Neutrality	Three Views of Heaven	Two Views of Foreknowledge

Some begin to doubt, wondering how they are ever going to know what is true. Moreover, many have misrepresented just how difficult and complex the Bible is, suggesting that it is easy to understand. The Danish philosopher Søren Kierkegaard offered a similarly provocative diagnosis: "The matter is quite simple. **The bible is very easy to understand**. But we Christians are a bunch of scheming swindlers. We pretend to be unable to understand it because we know very well that the minute we understand, we are obliged to act accordingly." If a churchgoer is sitting in the pews hearing how easy the Bible is to understand and at the same time struggling to understand it, this alone could be so overwhelming; it could contribute to a bout of depression. One might ask, "If the Bible is easy to understand and I cannot understand it, what does that say about me?" Relax; take a deep breath, the Bible is not even close to being easy to understand. Those who make such claims are likely the ones that are furthest from having a correct understanding of it. Even the inspired apostle Peter stated that he found the apostle Paul's letters 'difficult to understand.' (2 Pet. 3:16) If the Bible is so easy to understand, how on earth can Dr. Craig S. Keener (Ph.D., Duke University), pen a four-volume commentary on the book of Acts alone, which has 4640 pages?

Keeping the truth from people will inevitably lead to a spiritual shipwreck. Religious leaders can no longer hide the truth from their flock. There are several thousand Bible difficulties from Genesis to Revelation. Bible critics call these mistakes, errors, and contradictions. These would have never been discussed in our church 20-years ago because elders and pastors did not see the need for dealing with such hot topics, nor were they qualified to do so. Occasionally, in the 1980s, a flock member might happen upon a book in a store that attacked the Bible and the Christian faith, walking its reader through many of these so-called mistakes, errors, and contradictions. The Christian end up being heartbroken, keeping these doubts bottled up inside, falling away from the faith eventually. Some had even gone to the pastor or elder, showing them the book, who then blew it off by saying, "Why are you feeding your mind on such a book? This is simply a bunch of lies spread by false teachers." Of course, the pastor or elder was unable to explain how any of the Bible difficulties were lies. So few Christians were lost to this danger that it was felt that there was no need to talk about Bible difficulties, how many tens of thousands of different denominations there are the different views on all of the Bible doctrines, and the like.

However, the internet has exploded into the lives of every Christian; even the elderly is texting their friends. There is access to social media sites such as Facebook, Twitter, YouTube Pinterest, LinkedIn, Google + and dozens of others. There are now over 2 billion social media users worldwide, and more than half (52 percent) of those use two or more social media sites. Thus, the proverbial cat is out of the bag, or the beans have been spilled, meaning that the secret has been revealed unintentionally.

The flood of books, movies, and media by the Bible critics is so pervasive that we now have universities that are apologetic universities. **Christian apologetics** [Greek: *apologia*, "verbal defense, speech in defense"] is a field of **Christian theology** that endeavors to offer a reasonable and sensible basis for the **Christian faith**, defending the faith against objections. It is reasoning from the Scriptures, explaining and proving, as one instructs in sound doctrine, many times having to overturn false reasoning before he can plant the seeds of truth. It can also be earnestly contending for the faith and saving one from losing their faith, as they have begun to doubt. Moreover, it can involve rebuking those who contradict the truth. It is being prepared to make a defense to anyone who asks the Christian evangelist for a reason for the hope that is in him or her. – Jude 1.3, 21-23; 1 Pet 3.15; Acts 17:2-3; Titus 1:9.

The Truth Will Set You Free

The truth is,

- The Bible is a very complex and deep book, which 's hard to understand, but we have excellent study tools today, and anyone wanting to understand it, need only to buy out the time.

- There are over 41,000 different denominations, and all are not the truth and the way. In fact, many are false. However, it is true that one or more may be the truth and the way. Alternatively, it may be that it is true that there are many true Christians in some denominations, which Jesus will unite before the end comes.
- It is true that every Bible doctrine has more than one view, but not all are true. However, it is also true that the meaning of each of those doctrines is found in God's Word and only needs to be discovered.
- It is true that salvation is open to everyone. However, it is also true that few will find it because most are too lazy to buy out the time to study.
- It is true that God wants everyone to be saved. However, it is also true that he is interested only in saving those with a receptive heart.

The Problem You Face In Finding the One True Christian Church

The answer lies below but first, let us do a short review first. There are 41,000 different denominations today, all teaching different doctrinal positions than the other, many of which contradict the others. The divisiveness would never work in an effort to fulfill the great commission of making disciples. What if we just singled out the Baptist church as our test case. There are over well 50,000 Baptist churches in the United States of America. There are literally 61 different Baptist divisions, i.e., subdivision denominations within the Baptist Church. Yes, they all believe differently as well. What if we just select one of this subdivision denominations, will we finally find a oneness of mind and teachings? No. Why? Another divisive problem exists. The Baptist churches as a whole are autonomous, which means that every individual church has the freedom to act independently and teach differently than the others do. The irony is, they will argue that they are in agreement when it comes to the so-called salvation doctrines. Yet, this is not true because every one of the so-called salvation doctrines has anywhere from two to four different positions or views.

Zanesville, Ohio has eleven Baptist churches, in a community of 150,000 people. What if all eleven Baptist churches decided independently that they were going to go out and evangelize the community to make disciples? How could that even work? Suppose an unbeliever is visited by several different subdivision Baptist denominations and is told different views about the same doctrine? How is the unbeliever going to take

Christianity seriously with such division as this? Moreover, we have other problems that we have not even addressed.

Press on to Maturity

Hebrews 5:13-6:1 Updated American Standard Version (UASV)

¹³ For everyone who partakes of milk is unacquainted with the word of righteousness, for he is an infant. ¹⁴ But solid food belongs to the mature, to those who through practice have their discernment trained to distinguish between good and evil. **6** Therefore, leaving behind the elementary doctrine about the Christ, let us press on to maturity, not laying again a foundation of repentance from dead works and faith in God,

The problem of biblical illiteracy is well known but truly ignored. 90% of Christians are biblically illiterate in that they cannot explain the foundational doctrines of the faith or defend the Word of God as inspired, fully inerrant, and authoritative. Yes, they know some cute Bible stories and some Bible principles. This problem has existed for over a hundred years, and nothing has truly been done to address it. Then, we couple biblical illiteracy with the fact that **almost no Christians are being trained** to make disciples in their churches. Thus, we have 41,000 different denominations all teaching different doctrinal positions. We have tens of thousands of churches in the same denomination broken off into different sub-divisional denominations, and even a single subdivision has autonomous churches that believe differently, and the individual church has members that believe differently, with 90% being biblically illiterate and having no evangelism training. How do we fix that atrocious problem, so as to carry out the Great Commission?

How to Recognize a Real Church

A number of Christian denominations assert that they alone represent the one true church – the church to which Jesus gave his authority to the Great Commission. Some pastors have tried to answer this question and this issue, what is it that sets the one true church apart from the others? One offered the answer, 'the true Church is identified by fellowship, caring, and sharing, these are the most important aspects of true Christianity.' Sadly, think about this, you can find "fellowship, caring, and sharing" in drinking establishments, a social club, that is, in hundreds of places within society, these characteristics can be found.

How do you identify true Christianity? There was a study done with churchgoers a few years ago where they shared what was most important to them in a church that attracts them to become a member. The following mundane things were most important to these churchgoers: Number one was parking, number two was a nursery, number three was the style, followed by comfort, music, air conditioning, friendliness, and so on. Again, what should How to Interpret the Bible-1you look for in the one true church and what should it be? There is a very clear biblical answer. There is only one issue that makes a church or a denomination the one true church or denomination.

How does the Christian congregation who gather together handle Scripture? That is the only identifying mark that you need to concern yourself with. How do they handle the Word of God? The apostle Paul exhorted young Timothy, "¹⁵ Do your best to present yourself to God as one approved, a workman who does not need to be ashamed, **rightly handling**[17] **the word of truth.**" (2 Tim. 2:15) What do they believe about the Bible? Do they believe it is the inspired,[18] fully inerrant,[19] authoritative[20] Word of God? What do they believe the Bible teaches? How does the Bible form their living, preaching, and their teaching?

Psalm 119:161-165 Updated American standard Version (UASV)

¹⁶¹ Princes persecute me without cause,
　　but my heart stands **in awe of your words.**
¹⁶² **I rejoice at your word**
　　like one who finds great spoil.
¹⁶³ I hate and abhor falsehood,
　　but **I love your law.**
¹⁶⁴ Seven times a day I praise you
　　for your righteous judgments.
¹⁶⁵ Abundant peace belongs to those **loving your law,**
　　and for them there is no stumbling block.

Does your church stand 'in awe of God's Word'? The truest identifying marker of the true church is that it is the gathering of people that are in awe of the Word of God. We are to love God's Word above all else. As Isaiah said, we are to *tremble at the Word of God*. The church today has fragmented to the point of failure. Look at the so-called Christian nations and their moral decline over the past one hundred years. **The first step** to the failure of the church is that we have been on the path of eliminating the Bible out of the public discourse, **then step two** was to reverse morality (Isaiah 5, turn bitter into sweet and sweet into bitter, light into dark and

---

[17] Or *accurately handling* the word of truth; *correctly teaching* the word of truth
[18] https://christianpublishinghouse.co/2017/09/26/chicago-statement-on-biblical-hermeneutics/
[19] https://christianpublishinghouse.co/2017/09/26/chicago-statement-on-biblical-inerrancy-with-exposition/
[20] https://christianpublishinghouse.co/2017/09/26/inerrancy-of-the-scripture/

dark into light, and good into bad and bad into good). Now, the Christian is to no longer affirm the sin of homosexuality or the sin of immorality. The church has flipped morality so that what is biblically bad is now socially good and acceptable and the Bible is just a dated book that outlawed things in a different time and culture and does not really apply to us today.

Liberal-progressive and moderate Christianity has taken the driver's seat of the car of Christendom and has conservative Christianity riding in the back seat, if not the trunk. The liberal-progressive mindset that homosexuality is an acceptable alternative lifestyle,[21] the belief that abortion is acceptable under certain circumstances,[22] the belief that it is acceptable for woman to teach the church[23] when the apostle Paul under inspiration clearly says that they cannot, the belief that the Bible is nothing more than a book by man, and inspiration is not being led by "Holy Spirit," but simply being moved to pen something extraordinary, no different than a Shakespeare or even a John Grisham novel. Therefore, they accept the Bible as being full of errors, and that Adam and Eve are nothing more than allegorical (fictional) persons. Then there are the gender-inclusive translators, who remove masculine pronouns for gender-neutral ones.[24]

These ones fail to understand this: to deviate, in any way, from the pattern, or likeness of how God brought his Word into existence, merely opens the Bible up to a book that reflects the age and time of its readers. If we allow the Bible to be altered because the progressive woman's movement feels offended by masculine language or that women cannot teach the church, it will not be long before the Bible gives way to the homosexual communities being offended by God's Words in the book of Romans; so modern translations will then tame that language, so as to not cause offense. I am certain that we thought that we would never see the day of two men, or two women being married by priests, but that day has been upon us for some time now. In fact, the American government is debating whether to change the definition of marriage. Therefore, I would suggest that the liberal readers do not take my warning here as radicalism, but more as reality.

The third step is the church has been demanding tolerance, with the fourth step being that we are to be intolerant of those who are not tolerant, with **the final step** being persecution. There has long been persecution of Christianity, but now we are moving toward the persecution of

---

[21] https://christianpublishinghouse.co/2016/10/14/the-bibles-viewpoint-of-homosexuality/
[22] https://christianpublishinghouse.co/2016/11/10/does-abortion-show-respect-for-life/
[23] https://christianpublishinghouse.co/2017/01/03/women-in-the-pulpit/
[24] https://christianpublishinghouse.co/2016/11/08/gender-inclusive-language-in-bible-translation/

conservative Christianity by the world while liberal and moderate Christianity gets a pass.

Facing the Challenge of Finding the One True Church

The church can only fail in one way. It has **failed to be biblical.** The apostle Paul used the word Greek noun *epignosis* and the Greek verb *epignosko* a total of 24 times. In the New Testament, the verb (*epignosko*) occurs 42 times while the noun (*epignosis*) occurs 20 times. **Accurate Knowledge:** (Gr. *epignosis*) A strengthened or intensified form of *gnosis* (*epi*, meaning "additional"), meaning, "true," "real," "full," "complete" or "accurate," depending upon the context. Paul and Peter alone use *epignosis*. – Rom. 1:28; Eph. 1:17; Phil. 1:9; Col. 1:9-10; 1 Tim 2:4. If the church has an accurate knowledge of the Scriptures and is faithful to the Word of God, it cannot fail. If the church lives by and proclaims an accurate knowledge of the word of God, it does not fail. The Father accomplishes his will and purposes through his Word.

Psalm 143:8 Updated American Standard Version (UASV)

⁸ Let me hear in the morning of your loyal love,
 for I trust you.
Teach me the way in which I should walk,
 for to you I lift up my soul.

If we are going to be steadfast as we stand firm in our loyalty to God and his word, not the trends of the world, not the current cultural setting, we need to clearly and fully understand God's view on the matter and be determined to remain loyal to his ways. King David prayed to the Father,

Psalm 143:5, 10 Updated American Standard Version (UASV)

⁵ I remember the days of old;
 I **meditate on** all your doings;
 I **ponder** the work of your hands.

¹⁰ **Teach me** to do your will,
 for you are my God;
Let your good Spirit **lead me**
 on level ground.

David did not rely on his own ideas of what he thought, felt, or believed, or the urgings of another; but rather, he was eager to be taught by the Father. David meditated on or pondered all of the activities of the Father and focused his thinking on the work of God's own hands. We to can discern the will of the Father as well by have a regular personal study of the Bible that is beyond some simple Bible reading schedule, where we can meditate on the many Biblical accounts of the Father's dealings with humans. Just how important is the will of the Father?

Matthew 7:21-23 Updated American Standard Version (UASV)

[21] "Not everyone **[so-called Christians]** who says to me, 'Lord, Lord,' will enter the kingdom of heaven, but the one **[genuine Christian] who does the will of my Father** who is in heaven. [22] On that day many **[so-called Christians]** will say to me, 'Lord, Lord, did we **[so-called Christians]** not prophesy in your name, and cast out demons in your name, and do many mighty works in your name?' [23] And then I will declare to them **[so-called Christians]**, 'I never knew you; depart from me, you who practice lawlessness.'

1 John 2:15-17 Updated American Standard Version (UASV)

[15] Do not love the world or the things in the world. If anyone loves the world, the love of the Father is not in him. [16] For all that is in the world, the lust of the flesh and the lust of the eyes and the boastful pride of life, is not from the Father, but is from the world. [17] The world is passing away, and its lusts; but the one **[genuine Christian] who does the will of God** remains forever.

The only way that a church can fail is to fail to be biblical. Yes, the church needs to have a strategy to meet the needs of the modern Christian, to market to the unbeliever and believer, to connect with different cultures. However, under accurate knowledge, if it remains biblical in doing these things, it will not fail. Most of the churches today have really failed to be biblical.

Do Not Give Up in Your Walk with God!

Hebrews 12:1 Updated American Standard Version (UASV)

12 Therefore, since we have so great a cloud of witnesses surrounding us, let us also lay aside every weight and the sin which so easily entangles us, and let us run with endurance the race that is set before us,

One would not argue that the times we now live in are truly difficult, as they are violent in the extreme, designed to cater to our fleshly side, and both parents must work just to get by. All of this is by design, to cause Christians to take their eye off the one assignment that Jesus gave us. (Matt 24:14; 28:19-20; Ac 1:8) The words of the apostle Paul in the book of Hebrews is ever applicable to us as well, as we too need to **lay aside every weight, and sin which clings so closely, run with endurance the race that is set before us.**

"**Lay aside every weight**" is a reference to the Greek and Roman athletic games. "In the context of running, it could refer to burdensome clothing or excess body weight. Therefore, believers are to run the Christian race with endurance, laying aside those things that bind or weigh us down."[25] What type of weight could hinder us in the race that is set before us? We would want to set aside any constant thinking about a particular matter or persistent interest in fame or making as a reputation for ourselves, money, immoral or violent entertainment, excessive travel for pleasure,[26] and other material pursuits that can affect our thinking. – 1 John 2:15-17.

Constant thinking about or persistent interest, however, can wear us out emotionally, physically, and spiritually, affecting our trust in God. Paul

---

[25] Clinton E. Arnold, Zondervan Illustrated Bible Backgrounds Commentary Volume 4: Hebrews to Revelation., 75 (Grand Rapids, MI: Zondervan, 2002).

[26] There is nothing wrong with traveling more when you are retired, or even taking a vacation once or twice a year with your family up unto the time of retirement. However, the key word is "excessive." If John Smith truly believed that he was going to receive everlasting life; then, this life should be used to almost entirely to carry out the work Christians were given (Matt 28:19-20). Let us play with the belief and reality of everlasting life. The 70-80 years that we now live is what, when we think of say several hundred billion trillion years that lies ahead in our everlasting life. If a true believer saw it that way, this Great Commission of preaching, teaching, and making disciples would be taken more seriously. Here is how we should view pleasure and entertainment, as a means to recuperate, before getting back to our Great Commission. The commission is called great for a reason, and the analogy I gave for John smith, is like one piece of sand, in comparison to all of the sand on all of the planets in the 125 billion universes. That piece of sand, our 70-80 years of life now is not even on the scale of significance. My comment was for the wealthy Christian family, who travels for pleasure, **excessively.**

talks about how a lack of faith is "**sin which clings so closely.**" Imperfect humans, even Christians with the new personality and mind of Christ, have a propensity for finding themselves in periods of temporary weakness of faith. In these moments, they tend to act contrary to the Spirit's lead, through deception, human weaknesses, setting their hearts on other things, which in turn grieves the Holy Spirit, ending with their stumbling spiritually.

As to '**running with endurance,**' a Greek-English lexicon explains the Greek verb for "the capacity to hold out or bear up in the face of difficulty, patience, endurance, fortitude, steadfastness, perseverance."[27] Regarding the Greek noun for "endurance," *New Testament Words* says, "It is the spirit which can bear things, not simply with resignation, but with blazing hope; it is not the spirit [mental disposition] which sits statically enduring in one place, but the spirit which bears things because it knows that these things are leading to a goal of glory; it is not the patience which grimly waits for the end, but the patience which radiantly waits for the dawn ... It is the quality which keeps a man on his feet with his face to the wind. It is the virtue which can transmute the hardest trial into glory because beyond the pain it sees the goal."[28] Endurance empowers one to be steadfast if the face of hurdles and adversities all the while maintaining hope.

Pay Much Closer Attention

Hebrews 2:1 Updated American Standard Version (UASV)

2 For this reason we must pay much closer attention to the things that have been heard, so that we do not drift away from it.

What and where was the very first Christian congregation? It was the Jerusalem Christian congregation, founded right after Pentecost of 33 C.E. It was made up of the 12 apostles, Jesus brothers James and Jude, Mark who wrote the Gospel that bears his name, and hundreds of other Jews that personally knew Jesus, many traveling with him. You can only imagine how spiritually strong that congregation must have been. (Acts 2:44-47; 4:32-34; 5:41; 6:7) However, some 31 years later in 61-64 C.E., the congregation had grown tired and apathetic. Some were drifting away (2:1), others were falling away (6:6) or willfully begging off or turning away (12:25), while other had become sluggish (6:12) and some were shrinking back (10:39) from the truth that they had known from the beginning. How could this have happened? One resource wrote,

---

[27] William Arndt, Frederick W. Danker and Walter Bauer, A Greek-English Lexicon of the New Testament and Other Early Christian Literature, 3rd ed., 1039 (Chicago: University of Chicago Press, 2000).

[28] William Barclay, *New Testament Words.* 144-5 (Louisville: Westminster Press, 1974).

The persons addressed were in the mental and spiritual condition common in every age of the Christian church, a condition of languor [laziness] and weariness, of disappointed expectations, deferred hopes, conscious failure and practical unbelief. They were Christians but had slender appreciation of the glory of their calling, misconstrued their experience, and had allowed themselves to drift away from boldness and hope and intensity of faith.[29]

The comment from above, "the mental and spiritual condition common in every age of the Christian church," is the reason, we are going to review what the author of Hebrews wrote, to pull that first Christian congregation out of their spiritual stupor. The first seven years of Christianity, from 29 C.E., when the founder Jesus Christ was baptized, to 36 C.E., when the first Gentile was baptized, the Christian congregation was made up of Jews only. Some of these ones were very slow in getting over that there was a new way to God, through Jesus Christ. One must keep in mind that the only way for 1,500 years to be in an approved relationship with God was through the Israelite nation and the Mosaic Law. The system of worship that they had known throughout their entire life was now replaced with a new one. They had, under the old Jewish system, an extraordinary system of worship, priesthood, regular sacrifices, and a temple in Jerusalem that could be viewed as the ninth wonder of the world. Many Jewish Christians were unable to make the transition, as they walked aimlessly because of an inability to see how the Christian system was better than the Jewish system of the past, failing to get in the race for life.

Romans 10:4 Updated American Standard Version (UASV)

⁴ For Christ is the end of the law to everyone who believes.

Colossians 2:13-16 Updated American Standard Version (UASV)

¹³ And you, who were dead in your trespasses and the uncircumcision of your flesh, God made alive together with him, having forgiven us all our trespasses, ¹⁴ having canceled out the certificate of debt consisting of decrees against us, which was hostile to us; and he has taken it out of the way, having nailed it to the cross.[30] ¹⁵ having disarmed the rulers and authorities, he made a public display of them openly, triumphing over them by it.[31]

---

[29] W. Robertson Nicoll, The Expositor's Greek New Testament, Volume Four, 236 (Peabody: Hendrickson, 2002).
[30] **σταυρός stauros**; from the same as *2476; an upright stake*, hence *a cross* (the Rom. instrument of crucifixion):—cross(27).–NASB Dictionaries
[31] i.e. the cross; it could also be rendered *through him*

Let no Man Pass Judgment on You Based on Misinterpretation

¹⁶ Therefore let no man judge you about what you eat and drink or about the observance of a festival or of the new moon or of a sabbath day.³²

What about today, with Christians coming out of the world into the Christian congregation, is it not similar? The world is full of wonderment, power leaders, exciting innovations, scientific advancements, stimulating opportunities, and it is specifically designed to lure the unsuspecting one into its ways of thinking, and to retain them once they have them, as well as pull them back in if they ever choose to leave. It has generated a generation of **selfish, me-first people** that set aside God's Word, because they develop a wall of disbelief, setting impossible standards for the Bible while lowering the standards of secularism,³³ which enables them to feel good about being in the world or returning to the world. Then, there are the Christians who are **halfhearted**, having little enthusiasm, interest, support, or conviction in their worship of God. (Ps 119:113; Rev. 3:16)

Finally, there are those, who possess "**a double heart**" (Literally "a heart and a heart").³⁴ (Ps 12:2) In other words, these ones, go to every congregation meeting, are very active in their congregation, and at the same time, they are living a very worldly life outside of the congregation. It might be that they are materialistic, or they are unclean morally (1 Pet 2:12; He 4:13; 1 Cor. 6:9-11), mentally (Phil 4:8; Matt 15:18-20), in speech (Eph. 4:25, 29, 31; 5:3; Rev 21:8), and so on. They may lie, gamble, or steal by cheating on their taxes, or dishonest business practices. (Pro 6:16-19; Cols 3:9, 10) They may have fits of anger and are abusive to their wife, or children. (Ps 11:5; Proverbs 22:24, 25) They may be heavy drinkers and drunkards, which leads to their household problems. (1 Cor. 5:11-13; 1 Tim. 3:8) These ones are those who are deceptively presenting themselves as one thing to the Christian congregation while living an entirely different life outside of the congregation. – Matthew 15:7, 8.

So again, we revisit Paul's words to this Jewish congregation, "**Therefore, we must pay much closer attention** to what we have heard, lest we **drift away** from it." (Heb. 2:1)

Therefore is an adverb that introduces a statement that is a consequence of the previous statement. Chapter 1 of Hebrews was/is about

---

³² Or *days*
³³ Secularism is the rejection of religion or its exclusion from a philosophical or moral system.
³⁴ Footnote, Lexham English Bible

the supremacy of God's Son. Chapter 3 is similarly about Jesus being greater than Moses while chapter 4 demonstrates that Jesus is a superior high priest than in the Aaronic priesthood, and chapters 5 through 7 cover the superiority of Jesus to Melchizedek.[35] Thus, the "therefore," that begins chapter 2 is expressing that there is a serious need to consider the greatness of Christ and to learn more about Jesus. However, they needed to **pay much closer attention** to what we have heard, better appreciating the superiority of Jesus, and to negate the impressive Jewish system that had been their way for so long.

The idea of **drifting away** was a reference to ship sailing, which was a common mode of transportation in the first-century C.E. Roman Empire. If the captain of a ship does not keep his mind on the wind and current, he will risk running his ship past a safe harbor and onto rocky seashore. These Jewish Christians needed to pull themselves out of their apathetic stupor. In the same way, if we are not heeding the Word of God, by way of a regular, deeply personal and congregational Bible study, we too will drift ashore, experiencing spiritual shipwreck. Just like a captain, who is not paying attention, we may not wake up until it is too late.

An Evil and Unbelieving Heart

Hebrews 3:12-13 Updated American Standard Version (UASV)

¹² Take care, brothers, lest there be in any of you an evil, **heart of unbelief**, leading you to **fall away** from the living God. ¹³ But exhort one another every day, as long as it is called "today," that none of you may be **hardened** by the deceitfulness of sin.

We cannot remain "pure in heart" (Matt 5:8) if we develop an evil **heart of unbelief**. An evil heart of unbelief [kardia ponēra apistias]) is "a remarkable combination. Heart ([kardia]) is common in the LXX[36] (about 1,000 times), but "evil heart" only twice in the O.T. (Jer. 16:12; 18:12). [Apistias] is more than mere unbelief, here rather disbelief, refusal to believe, genitive case describing the evil heart marked by disbelief which is no mark of intelligence then or now.[37]

What beliefs have the world of mankind spread that would undermine one's faith in God to such an extent? **(1) Evolution** is the theoretical process by which all species develop from earlier forms of life. **(2) Relativism** is the

---

[35] A priest and king of Salem who blessed Abraham, and in essence, blessed the Aaronic priesthood that was in his loins.

[36] LXX is the Greek Septuagint, a Greek translation of the Hebrew Bible made between 280 to 150 B.C.E. to meet the needs of Greek-speaking Jews outside Palestine.

[37] A.T. Robertson, Word Pictures in the New Testament, Heb 3:12 (Nashville, TN: Broadman Press, 1933).

belief that concepts such as right and wrong, goodness and badness, or truth and falsehood are not absolute but change from culture to culture and situation to situation. **(3) Limited inerrancy**, as opposed to full inerrancy, has caused many to lose their faith. Full inerrancy affirms that the original Scriptures contained no errors at all. Limited inerrancy, on the other hand, affirms that Scripture is without error in matters of salvation doctrine, but not history, science, or geography. **(4) Secularism** is the rejection of religion or its exclusion from a philosophical or moral system. **(5) Atheism** is disbelief in the existence of God or deities. **(6) Biblical criticism** is known as the historical-critical method of Bible study, such as the study of historical criticism, literary criticism, form criticism, tradition criticism, redaction criticism, structuralist criticism, among others. This is known as the new way of biblical interpretation, and it undermines the trustworthiness of Scripture, a pseudo-scholarship. **(7) Empiricism** is the philosophical belief that all knowledge is derived from the experience of the senses to the exclusion of revelatory knowledge, such as the Word of God. **(8) Existentialism** is a philosophical movement begun in the 19th century that denies that the universe has any intrinsic meaning or purpose. It requires people to take responsibility for their own actions and shape their own destinies. **(9) Pragmatism** is the position that "those beliefs are true which it is expedient for us to act upon and believe." **(10) Religious Liberalism** is a movement in Protestantism stressing intellectual freedom and the moral content of Christianity over the doctrines of traditional theology. The abandonment of "the traditional view of authority and truth in order to substitute a newer source of authority, typically based on experience or intellectual conclusions."[38] This list could go on for some time, but I believe you have gotten the point. The Word of God, true Christianity, and truth has been under an ever-greater attack throughout the 20th and into the 21st century, the pinnacle of the enlightenment age that got its start in the late 17th century with René Descartes. We must not let ourselves be caught off guard by such death-dealing beliefs.

What is the result of an unbelieving heart that has been infected with the thinking of man? It leads one to **fall away** (Gr., *apostenai*, "to stand off") from the living God. Just how serious is this? You will notice that earlier, Paul spoke of '**drifting away**' because of not paying attention to one's spiritual needs. (Heb. 2:1; Matt 5:3) However, the Greek term *apostenai* rendered "fall away," which is more of a willful drawing away, means "to stand off" and is related to the word "apostasy." This is standing off from the truth that was once accepted. It signifies a willful and

---

[38] Hindson, Ed (2008-05-01). The Popular Encyclopedia of Apologetics (Kindle Locations 11777-11778). Harvest House Publishers. Kindle Edition.

purposeful resisting, withdrawing, and abandoning, with a measure of disdain added. One New Testament word study book offered,

> The word "departing" deserves special attention. It is *aphistemi* which is made up of *apo* "off," and *histemi* "to stand," the compound word meaning "to stand off from." This was exactly the position of these Hebrews. They were standing aloof from the living God. The idea is not that of departing, but of standing off from. Our word "apostasy" is derived from a form of this Greek word. Apostasy is defined as the act of someone who has previously subscribed to a certain belief, and who now renounces his former professed belief in favor of some other, which is diametrically opposed to what he believed before. In other words, his new belief is not merely a new system of faith, but one, which at every point negates his former belief.[39]

As was stated, the **drifting away** of Hebrews 2:1 is the result of being inattentive to one's spiritual needs, and bears repeating. In that circumstance, there is no real effort involved to end up spiritually shipwrecked. However, this **falling away** is the result of someone taking action. This one is willfully "falling away from the living God." Why? Paul gives us the answer, namely, an evil, **heart of unbelief**. This evil heart of unbelief is **not** the result of not being a student of the Bible, nor having sufficient knowledge of Scripture, or even an incorrect understanding of Scripture. Paul goes on to quote the occasion of the Israelites at Exodus 15, which is also referenced in Psalm 95:8, "do not harden your hearts as in the rebellion" at Meribah. The Israelites had enjoyed Jehovah's God's love, protection, and saw his "works for forty years" while in the wilderness. (Heb. 3:7-11) However, these very ones hardened their hearts against him.

In the same sense, Christians today, need to "consider how to stir up one another to love and good works, not neglecting to meet together, as is the habit of some, but encouraging one another" (Heb. 10:24-25), so that "none of you may be **hardened** by the deceitfulness of sin." What have we learned thus far? **(1)** We do not want to neglect personal Bible study. **(2)** We should be well prepared for congregation meetings **(3)** We should have mercy on those who have begun to doubt because they have fed their minds on literature from Bible critics; and we should have the ability to reason from the Scriptures, to help them overcome their doubts. **(4)** In addition, we stir up one another to love and good works, not neglecting to meet together.

---

[39] Kenneth S. Wuest, Wuest's Word Studies from the Greek New Testament: For the English Reader, Heb 3:12 (Grand Rapids: Eerdmans, 1997).

Am I suggesting that Christians should never read a book by a Bible critic? No. However, would you venture into any unsafe place in life without preparing for it first? Let me offer an illustration. A prosecuting attorney goes to the best law school in the US, studies under one of the greatest legal minds, and he may have 30-years of experience. He puts on the state's case, and you are mesmerized by his knowledge of the law, the skill with which he presents it, and you find the defendant guilty as you sit in the jury box. However, one thing is missing. What? You have yet to hear the defense attorney. Do you now have blinders to the point that it does not matter? ("you" here is plural, not you personally) The irony is, once the defense attorney gets up and presents his case, you are so stunned by the evidence that he presents, that you have now completely changed your position.

This is what would happen if you read the Bible critics book first. You would feel that it really cast doubts about the existence of a personal God, who created everything, and that such a being inspires the Bible is no longer true. Then, you read an apologetic Bible scholar's book that deals with the same issues, say that of Dr. William Lane Craig, concluding you did not have all the facts, and now feel saddened because you doubted in the first place. What I recommend is that you read the apologetic Bible scholar's book first, like putting in a bulletproof vest, and then read the Bible critic's book if you so desire.

Do Not Shrink Back to Destruction

Hebrews 10:39 Updated American Standard Version (UASV)

[39] But we are not of those who **shrink back** and are destroyed, but of those who have faith and preserve their souls.

Paul closes this section with serious confidence that they "are not of those who **shrink back** and are destroyed." Today, true Christians live in a time like no other and are under a constant bombardment from the world that surrounds us. Like Paul and the Jewish Christians, who heeded his counsel, we too do not want to shrink back to destruction. This does not mean that we will never have a moment of fear, as we are susceptible to being afraid like any other imperfect human. The Greek *hupostello* means "'to draw back, withdraw,' perhaps a metaphor for lowering a sail and so slackening the course, and hence of being remiss in holding the truth."[40] A Christian with faith, will not 'draw back or withdraw' from their commitment to God's will and purposes, 'slacking off in their course.'

---

[40] W. E. Vine, Merrill F. Unger and William White, Jr., vol. 2, Vine's Complete Expository Dictionary of Old and New Testament Words, 180 (Nashville, TN: T. Nelson, 1996).

Regardless of what this wicked world, alienated from God throws at them, such as persecution, difficulties, health issues, or any other tribulation. They will face these head on, like the apostle Paul, who said, "For the sake of Christ, then, I am content with weaknesses, insults, hardships, persecutions, and calamities. For when I am weak, then I am strong." (2 Cor. 12:10) Yes, we must be steadfast in our service to God, as he is well aware of our limitations, and he makes allowances for these, "he remembers that we are dust." – Psalm 55:22; 103:14.

Do Not Grow Weary or Fainthearted

Hebrews 12:3 Updated American Standard Version (UASV)

³ For consider the one who endured such hostility by sinners against himself, so that you will not **grow weary in your souls and give up**.

> As we reflect on our own hardships, we need to assess carefully the endurance of Jesus. Jesus endured hostility from sinners that reached its climax at the cross. When you tend to let go, you can avoid faintheartedness and weariness by keeping your attention riveted upon Jesus. Jesus endured hostility from stubborn sinners. You have never faced such intense evil as did Jesus. His sterling example can stabilize us in our fear and concern.[41]

What is it that we are not to grow weary in your souls and give up from? What is it Satan would love us to get too tired to carry out? The answer is found in verses 1-2.

Hebrews 12:1-2 Updated American Standard Version (UASV)

12 Therefore, since we have so great a cloud of witnesses surrounding us, let us also lay aside every weight and the sin which so easily entangles us, and let us **run with endurance the race** that is set before us, ² **fixing our eyes on Jesus**, the author and perfecter of faith, who for the joy set before him endured the cross, despising the shame, and has sat down at the right hand of the throne of God.

Have you bought out the time to know why Jesus ever came to earth as a man in the first place? First, we can say that the Gospels are of his life and ministry. From this, you can see that his focus was on his ministry. Jesus came to earth as a man for three reasons. **(1)** Jesus said, "For this purpose, I was born, and for this purpose, I have come into the world—to bear witness to the truth." (John 18:37) **(2)** Peter said this to Christians, "For to

---

[41] Thomas D. Lea, *Hebrews, James*, vol. 10, Holman New Testament Commentary (Nashville, TN: Broadman & Holman Publishers, 1999), 219.

this you have been called, because Christ also suffered for you, leaving you an example, so that you might follow in his steps." (1 Pet. 2:21) **(3)** Jesus tells us this, "even as the Son of Man came not to be served but to serve, and to give his life as a ransom for many." (Matt. 20:28) Jesus came to leave us an example, for us to follow in his steps, which example is his ministry that he carried out to the Jews of his day, and we are to carry out to all people. (Matt. 28:19-20) The sad irony, there are really no churches within the 39,000 denominations that I am aware of based on my personal statistical surveys, which have even begun to carry out a similar message to the nations, so there is no real reason to be tired out from this work. Oh yes, they send out missionaries here and there, but the truth is, **all Christians** are responsible for preaching, teaching and making disciples. With or without the church, we need to make progress toward maturity and improve our ministry (evangelistic) skills, so as to carry out the Great Commission we were given.

BIBLICAL TRAINING ACADEMY

www.biblicaltrainingacademy.co
866-580-6125 Ext. #2

UPDATED AMERICAN STANDARD VERSION

www.uasvbible.org/donation
866-580-6125 Ext. #3

RECOMMENDED BOOKS

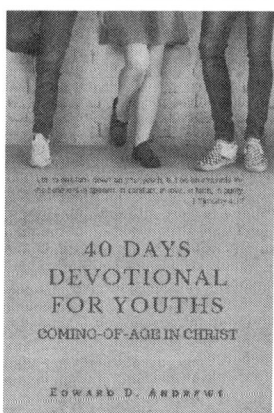

Bibliography

Akin, D. L. (2001). *The New American Commentary: 1, 2, 3 John.* Nashville, TN: Broadman & Holman .

Alden, R. L. (2001). *Job, The New American Commentary, vol. 11* . Nashville: Broadman & Holman Publishers.

Aldrich, C. J. (1981). *Lifestyle Evangelism.* Portland, OR: Multnoma Press.

Anders, M. (1999). *Holman New Testament Commentary: vol. 8, Galatians-Colossians* . Nashville, TN: Broadman & Holman Publishers.

Anders, M. (2005). *Holman Old Testament Commentary - Proverbs* . Nashville: B&H Publishing.

Anders, M., & Butler, T. (2002). *Holman Old Testament Commentary: Isaiah.* Nashville, TN: B&H Publishing.

Anders, M., & Lawson, S. (2004). *Holman Old Testament Commentary - Psalms: 11.* Grand Rapids: B&H Publishing.

Anders, M., & McIntosh, D. (2009). *Holman Old Testament Commentary - Deuteronomy.* Nashville: B&H Publishing.

Anders, M., & McIntosh, D. (2009). *Holman Old Testament Commentary - Deuteronomy.* Nashville: B&H Publishing.

Andrews, E. D. (2016). *THE CHRISTIAN APOLOGIST: Always Being Prepared to Make a Defense [Second Edition].* Cambridge, OH: Christian Publishing House.

Andrews, E. D. (2016). *THE EVANGELISM HANDBOOK: How All Christians Can Effectively Share God's Word in Their Community, [SECOND EDITION].* Cambridge, OH: Christian Publishing House.

Andrews, E. D. (2017). *CONVERSATIONAL EVANGELISM: Defending the Faith, Reasoning from the Scriptures, Explaining and Proving, Instructing in Sound Doctrine, and Overturning False Reasoning [Second Edition].* Cambridge, OH: Christian Publishing House.

Andrews, E. D. (2018). *CHRISTIAN APOLOGETIC EVANGELISM: Reaching Hearts with the Art of Persuasion.* Cambridge, OH: Christian Publishing House.

Andrews, E. D. (2018). *REASONING WITH THE WORLD'S VARIOUS RELIGIONS: Examining and Evangelizing Other Faiths.* Cambridge, OH: Christian Publishing House.

Andrews, E. D., & Overton, T. (2018). *THE GREAT TEACHER JESUS CHRIST: What Made Jesus Christ's Teaching, Preaching, Evangelism, and Apologetics Outstandingly Effective?* Cambridge, OH: Christian Publishing House.

Andrews, S. J., & Bergen, R. D. (2009). *Holman Old Testament Commentary: 1-2 Samuel.* Nashville: Broadman & Holman.

Archer, G. L. (1982). *New International Encyclopedia of Bible Difficulties, Zondervan's Understand the Bible Reference Series.* Zondervan Publishing House: Grand Rapids, MI.

Barker, K. L., & Bailey, W. (2001). *The New American Commentary: vol. 20, Micah, Nahum, Habakkuk, Zephaniah.* Nashville, TN: Broadman & Holman Publishers.

Bechtle, D. M. (2006). *Evangelism for the Rest of Us: Sharing Christ within Your Personality Style.* Grand Rapids, MI: Baker Books.

Benner, D. G., & Hill, P. C. (1985, 1999). *Baker Encyclopedia of Psychology and Counseling (Second Edition).* Grand Rapids: Baker Books.

Bercot, D. W. (1998). *A Dictionary of Early Christian Beliefs.* Peabody: Hendrickson.

Bergen, R. D. (1996). *The New American Commentary: 1-2 Samuel.* Nashville: Broadman & Holman.

Blomberg, C. (1992). *The New American Commentary: Matthew.* Nashville, TN: Broadman & Holman Publishers.

Boa, K., & Kruidenier, W. (2000). *Holman New Testament Commentary: Romans.* Nashville: Broadman & Holman.

Borchert, G. L. (2001). *The New American Commentary: John 1-11 .* Nashville, TN: Broadman & Holman Publishers.

Borchert, G. L. (2002). *The New American Commentary vol. 25B, John 12–21.* Nashville: Broadman & Holman Publishers.

Brand, C., Draper, C., & Archie, E. (2003). *Holman Illustrated Bible Dictionary: Revised, Updated and Expanded.* Nashville, TN: Holman.

Breneman, M. (1993). *The New American Commentary, vol. 10, Ezra, Nehemiah, Esther.* Nashville: Broadman & Holman Publishers.

Bromiley, G. W. (1986). *The International Standard Bible Encyclopedia (Vol. 1-4).* Grand Rapids, MI: William B. Eerdmans Publishing Co.

Bromiley, G. W., & Friedrich, G. (1964-). *Theological Dictionary of the New Testament, ed. Gerhard Kittel, vol. 4.* Grand Rapids, MI: Eerdmans.

Brooks, J. A. (1992). *The New American Commentary: Mark (Volume 23).* Nashville: Broadman & Holman Publishers.

Butler, T. C. (2000). *Holman New Testament Commentary: Luke.* Nashville, TN: Broadman & Holman Publishers.

Butler, T. C. (2005). *Holman Old Testament Commentary - Hosea, Joel, Amos, Obadiah, Jonah, Micah .* Nashville: Broadman & Holman Publishers.

Caba, T. e. (2007). *The Apologetics Study Bible: Real Questions, Straight Answers, Stronger Faith.* Nashville: Holman Bible Publishers.

Cole, R. D. (2000). *THE NEW AMERICAN COMMENTARY: Volume 3b Numbers.* Nashville: Broadman & Holman Publishers.

Coleman, R. E. (2010). *The Master Plan of Evangelism.* Grand Rapids, MI: Revell.

Cooper, L. E. (1994). *The New American Commentary, Ezekiel, vol. 17.* Nashville, TN: Broadman & Holman Publishers.

Cooper, R. (2000). *Holman New Testament Commentary: Mark.* Nashville: Broadman & Holman Publishers.

Easley, K. H. (1998). *Revelation, vol. 12, Holman New Testament Commentary.* Nashville, TN:: Broadman & Holman Publishers.

Elwell, W. A. (2001). *Evangelical Dictionary of Theology (Second Edition).* Grand Rapids: Baker Academic.

Elwell, W. A., & Beitzel, B. J. (1988). *Baker Encyclopedia of the Bible.* Grand Rapids, MI: Baker Book House.

Elwell, W. A., & Comfort, P. W. (2001). *Tyndale Bible Dictionary.* Wheaton: Tyndale House Publishers.

Gangel, K. O. (1998). *Holman New Testament Commentary: Acts.* Nashville, TN: Broadman & Holman Publishers.

Gangel, K. O. (2000). *Holman New Testament Commentary, vol. 4, John .* Nashville, TN: Broadman & Holman Publishers.

Gangel, K. O. (2001). *Holman Old Testament Commentary: Daniel.* Nashville: Broadman & Holman Publishers.

Gangel, K., & Anders, M. (2002). *Daniel, vol. 18, Holman Old Testament Commentary.* Nashville, TN: Broadman & Holman Publishers.

Garrett, D. A. (1993). *Proverbs, Ecclesiastes, Song of Songs, The New American Commentary, vol. 14.* Nashville: Broadman & Holman Publishers.

Garrett, D. A. (1993). *The New American Commentary: Vol. 14 (Proverbs, Ecclesiastes, Song of Songs).* Nashville: Broadman & Holman Publishers.

Geisler, D. a. (2009, 2014). *Conversational Evangelism.* EUGENE, OREGON: Harvest House Publishers.

George, T. (2001). *The New American Commentary: Galatians.* Nashville, TN: Broadman & Holman Publishers.

Green, M. (2004). *Evangelism in the Early Church.* Grand Rapids, MI: Eerdmans.

House, P. R. (2001). *The New American Commentary: 2 Kings.* Nashville: Broadman & Holman Publishers.

Larson, K. (2000). *Holman New Testament Commentary, vol. 9, I & II Thessalonians, I & II Timothy, Titus, Philemon.* Nashville, TN: Broadman & Holman Publishers.

Lea, T. D. (1999). *Holman New Testament Commentary: Hebrews, James.* Nashville, TN: Broadman & Holman Publishers.

Lea, T. D., & Griffin, H. P. (1992). *The New American Commentary, vol. 34, 1, 2 Timothy, Titus.* Nashville: Broadman & Holman Publishers.

MacArthur, J. F. (2011). *Evangelism: How to Share the Gospel Faithfully (MacArthur Pastor's Library).* Nashville, TN: Thomas Nelson.

Martin, D. M. (2001, c1995). *The New American Commentary 33 1, 2 Thessalonians.* Nashville, TN: Broadman & Holman.

Martin, G. S. (2002). *Holman Old Testament Commentary: Numbers.* Nashville: Broadman & Holman Publishers.

Mathews, K. A. (2001). *The New American Commentary vol. 1A, Genesis 1-11:26.* Nashville: Broadman & Holman Publishers.

Matthews, K. A. (2001). *The New American Commentary Vol. 1B, Genesis 11:27-50:26.* Nashville: Broadman and Holman Publishers.

McRaney, W. (2003). *The Art of Personal Evangelism.* Nashville: Broadman & Holman.

McRaney, W. (2003). *The Art of Personal Evangelism: Sharing Jesus in a Changing Culture.* Grand Rapids, MI: B&H Academic.

Melick, R. R. (2001). *The New American Commentary: Philippians, Colossians, Philemon, electronic ed., Logos Library System.* Nashville: Broadman & Holman Publishers.

Melick, R. R. (2001). *The New American Commentary: vol. 32, Philippians, Colissians, Philemon.* Nashville, TN : Broadman & Holman Publishers.

Miller, S. R. (1994). *Daniel, vol. 18, The New American Commentary.* Nashville:: Broadman & Holman Publishers.

Mounce, R. H. (2001). *The New American Commentary: Vol. 27 Romans.* Nashville, TN: Broadman & Holman Publishers.

Mounce, R. H. (2001, c1995). *Romans: The New American Commentary 27.* Nashville: Broadman & Holman.

Mounce, W. D. (2006). *Mounce's Complete Expository Dictionary of Old & New Testament Words.* Grand Rapids, MI: Zondervan.

Polhill, J. B. (2001). *The New American Commentary 26: Acts.* Nashville: Broadman & Holman Publishers.

Pratt Jr, R. L. (2000). *Holman New Testament Commentary: I & II Corinthians, vol. 7.* Nashville: Broadman & Holman Publishers.

Reid, A. (2009). *Evangelism Handbook: Biblical, Spiritual, Intentional, Missional.* Grand Rapids, MI: B&H Academic.

Reid, A. (2017). *Sharing Jesus without Freaking Out: Evangelism the Way You Were Born to Do It.* Grand Rapid, MI: B&H Academic.

Richardson, K. (1997). *The New American Commentary Vol. 36 James.* Nashville: Broadman & Holman Publishers.

Rooker, M. F. (2000). *The New American Commentary, vol. 3A, Leviticus.* Nashville: Broadman & Holman Publishers.

Rooker, M. F. (2001). *Leviticus: The New American Commentary.* Nashville: Broadman & Holman.

Rooker, M. F. (2005). *Holman Old Testament Commentary: Ezekiel.* Nashville: Broadman & Holman Publishers.

Schreiner, T. R. (2003). *The New American Commentary: 1, 2 Peter, Jude.* Nashville: Broadman & Holman.

Smith, G. (2007). *The New American Commentary: Isaiah 1-39, Vol. 15a.* Nashville, TN: B & H Publishing Group.

Smith, G. (2009). *The New American Commentary: Isaiah 40-66, Vol. 15b.* Nashville, TN: B&H Publishing.

Smith, W. (1890). *Smith's Dictionary of the Bible.* New York, NY: Hurd and Houghton, Cambridge Riverside Press.

Stein, R. H. (2001, c1992). *The New American Commentary: Luke.* Nashville, TN: Broadman & Holman.

Stiles, J. M. (2014). *Evangelism: How the Whole Church Speaks of Jesus (9marks: Building Healthy Churches).* Wheaton, IL: Crossway.

Story, D. (1999). *Engaging the Closed Minded: Presenting Your Faith to the Confirmed Unbeliever.* Grand Rapids, MI: Kregel Publications.

Stuart, D. K. (2006). *The New American Commentary: An Exegetical Theological Exposition of Holy Scripture EXODUS.* Nashville: Broadman & Holman.

Swanson, J. (1997). *Dictionary of Biblical Languages with Semantic Domains: Greek (New Testament).* Oak Harbor: Logos Research Systems.

Swanson, J. (1997). *Dictionary of Biblical Languages with Semantic Domains: Hebrew (Old Testament).* Oak Harbor: Logos Research Systems.

Taylor, R. A., & Clendenen, R. E. (2007). *The New American Commentary: Haggai, Malachi, , vol. 21A .* Nashville, TN: Broadman & Holman Publishers.

Vine, W. E., Unger, M. F., & White Jr., W. (1996). *Vine's Complete Expository Dictionary of Old and New Testament Words.* Nashville, TN: T. Nelson.

Vunderink, R. W., & Bromiley, G. W. (1979–1988). *The International Standard Bible Encyclopedia, Revised (, .* Grand Rapids, MI: Wm. B. Eerdmans.

Walls, D., & Anders, M. (1996). *Holman New Testament Commentary: I & II Peter, I, II & III John, Jude.* Nashville: Broadman & Holman Publishers.

Weber, S. K. (2000). *Holman New Testament Commentary, vol. 1, Matthew.* Nashville, TN: Broadman & Holman Publishers.

Wood, D. R. (1996). *New Bible Dictionary (Third Edition).* Downers Grove: InterVarsity Press.

Zodhiates, S. (2000, c1992, c1993). *The Complete Word Study Dictionary: New Testament.* Chattanooga: AMG Publishers.

Printed in Great Britain
by Amazon